DEADLY ANGEL

The Bizarre True Story of
Alaska's Killer Stripper

FRED ROSEN

HARPER

An Imprint of HarperCollins*Publishers*

The names of some individuals have been changed to preserve their anonymity. In some cases composite characters have been created in order to further preserve privacy. The goal in all cases was to protect people's privacy without damaging the integrity of the story.

HARPER

An Imprint of HarperCollins*Publishers*
10 East 53rd Street
New York, New York 10022-5299

Copyright © 2009 by Fred Rosen
ISBN 978-0-06-173398-7

First Harper paperback printing: July 2009

Printed in the United States of America

Visit Harper paperbacks on the World Wide Web at
www.harpercollins.com

10 9 8 7 6 5 4 3 2 1

A LETTER FROM BEYOND THE GRAVE

Don't dwell on my death. It was my time, and there is nothing that can change that. There are a few things that I would like you to do for me, though I hate to be vindictive in my death, but paybacks are hell.

First of all, pay all my debt with the insurance money. That I owe you. Then go on a nice vacation . . . act like I am there with you and do the things I would like to do. Lie on the beach, fish, relax. Two weeks minimum, but not much longer.

Gary Brooks would like to own the Togiak. Give it to him if you can, otherwise, sell it to him so that he can afford it. Owning the boat might make a difference in his life. . . .

Sorry about giving you all this stuff to do. I would have done it, but I wanted to make things work. I wanted to marry Mechele. If that would have happened, this would have all been destroyed. I have kept it as my "insurance policy." Use it! I'll rest easier. . . .

Make sure Mechele goes to jail for a long time, but visit her there. Tell her how much I really did (do) love her. Tell her you love her, and help her. She has a split personality, and the part I fell in love with is very beautiful. I really did want to marry her and make her dreams come true.

Love ya,
Kent

By Fred Rosen

Nonfiction

DEADLY ANGEL
WHEN SATAN WORE A CROSS
THERE BUT FOR THE GRACE OF GOD

*To Stewie, who would have loved having a book
about a stripper dedicated to him*

No man is above the law and no man is below it; nor do we ask any man's permission when we require him to obey it. Obedience to the law is demanded as a right, not asked as a favor.

Former Commissioner of the New York City Police,
President Theodore Roosevelt,
during his Third Annual Message to Congress,
December 7, 1903

DEADLY ANGEL

PART I
King of the Wild Frontier

Prologue

Alaska's about gold, plain and simple, and don't let anyone tell you otherwise.

Since 1897 when Thomas Edison's silent film of the *Passion Play* unspooled in Alaska and everywhere else, people have been going to the place looking for the yellow stuff in one form or another. There's lots of money involved. Where lots of money is involved there is always deceit, murder, and plenty of work for cops.

Detective Preston Wade walked around the red flags that the forensic team had already set up at the crime scene in the Alaskan bush. The first thing he noticed about the guy in the red jacket was that he had been shot with a .44 Magnum. Whoever had done the work had not bothered to clean up after himself. Instead, he had left behind three .44 caliber Magnum casings, marked by red flags, recovered nearby. By an amazing coincidence, the number of shell casings coincided with the bullet holes in the guy's body.

There were two in front, bloody and gaping, in the chest and cheek, characteristic of the powerful .44 Magnum ammunition. Turning the body, Wade saw the third yawning bullet hole in the back. Three shots total. The killer had wanted to be sure the job was done. But what was with the cheek wound?

Maybe the guy was shot in the back, whirled on impact, and the killer shot him in the chest and cheek, the latter while aiming for the head. Or maybe the cheek wound was more *personal*, meant as some sort of payback? Hard to say without further investigation, which was why Wade was there in the first place.

Preston Wade was a homicide detective with the Division of Alaska State Troopers, a part of the Alaska Department of Public Safety. Alaska has only five state police detachments to work a state of 663,267 square miles. Next to it, Texas is small, a mere 261,797 square miles. On the other hand, in 1996 Texas has 19,128,261 residents to Alaska's 605,212. That makes Alaska the least populated state in the Union, with about 1.1 residents per square mile.

A veteran detective, Wade had been with the state police since 1983, when Alaska set a modern high with eighty-one murders. Last year in 1995, homicides had gone down to fifty-five. That still left plenty of work for the five detachments. Wade worked out of Detachment E in Anchorage, 88.37 miles from the crime scene.

At the scene some things seemed apparent to his trained eye. There were no drag marks, or signs of a struggle. That indicated that the guy in the red jacket with three bullet holes in him had been shot and killed where he lay. Of course, someone could have carried him in there, dead, and then dumped the body, but if that happened there would definitely be footprints and likely other evidence for the crime scene technicians to process.

For the killer or killers, it made *sense*, a whole lot of *sense*. Killing a person off a rural road, in a rarely traversed section of the bush, heck, he could have been there for months, years, eternity without being discovered if not for the problem with the power line towering over his corpse. Wade shivered into his green wool greatcoat, a World War II survivor he had obtained for $19 from an army/navy store in Anchorage.

After pulling a pair of plastic gloves from the pockets, he donned them to physically search the body. Wade noticed that the victim's legs had curiously crossed in death. It was probably from the way he had fallen. There were no defensive wounds on his arms or hands. Once he had hit the ground, he was either already dead or very close to it. The autopsy should help answer some of those questions.

Well, he had seventy-two hours. The old saw that the first seventy-two hours of a murder investigation is the most important is absolutely true. It's during that time that cops like Wade have the best shot at getting the information that nails the murderer or murderers. Especially if you are dealing with two people, it could become rather difficult.

Wade had worked more than one homicide where there were two murderers. He didn't expect them to be standing around someplace waiting to be captured. Made no difference really. There is one essential element of criminal law that every state, including Alaska, has in common: there is no statute of limitations on murder.

Wade's job was to bring in the murderer. Sooner, of course, was preferred over later. Unfortunately, we don't always get everything we wish for.

April 27, 1996

The bore tide was coming in as Kent Leppink tooled his Dodge Omni out of the city. The power of the water was astonishing to watch.

Crashing through the narrow inlet of Turnagain Arm, the incoming edge of water rose to a full six-foot tidal wave, only to be met by the outgoing tide that smacked it down. It was sort of the way his emotions were running lately.

Leppink was familiar with tides. The thirty-six-year-old Michigan native captained his own seventy-five-foot tender, the *Togiak*. Under his command, the ship had already ferried more than a million pounds of fish from commercial fishing boats to the fish processors. But all was not well with the captain of the *Togiak*. The six-five, 195-pound bearded fisherman was having trouble with his twenty-three-year-old fiancée, Mechele Hughes.

It's hard to describe parents' reaction when their son

comes home and says, "Mom and Dad, I'm gonna marry a stripper." Leppink didn't do quite that, though he did call his parents to tell them of the engagement. He also did something else. Driving his car south out of Anchorage on Seward Highway, around the north shore of the Arm, stretching along the edge of the Chugach Mountain Range, he was secure in the knowledge that one way or another, he would get what he truly wanted, in life or in death. It was in the mail.

Between the mountain scenery and the bore tide, the drive was spectacular enough that all the travel brochures advertised it. Though he couldn't have missed it driving his Dodge Omni down the highway, Leppink didn't pay much attention to the scenery. He was more interested in the note on the front seat.

Dear Mechele,

The roof on your cabin in Hope is finished. It will not leak anymore. The fireplace has been cleaned but as he said, it will have to be redone in the next year or two. It is safe for you to use now. It also had all the locks changed and the key is under the stone by the tree, where the old key was. It has dead bolts now as well, so you will feel safe when you are there. The one key is universal and will fit all the door locks. I could not find someone willing to go to Hope to clean it though, so it will still be a little dusty. Also, the window screens are all fixed so there will be no mosquitos that will get in. I believe that they are coming out now and are very hungry for fair skin people such as us. I am glad that I bought it for you now. It does make a fine getaway. I think when you come back from there this weekend, I would like to spend a couple of days there myself, if that is okay. I need time to figure out where I am going with my life when I sell the house. I have been thinking of Australia, if the Costa Rica deal doesn't look inviting and I don't like it. I sure am going to miss you but I know if something happens or you become unhappy here, you will call me and we can spend time together wherever I am at. You know how much I would like that. I do wish you all the happiness and joy in the world. I am sure you will be happy and raise a fine family. I do hate going and loosing [sic] you in my life thought [sic]. Please be well, safe, and Happy. You guys enjoy your stay in the cabin this weekend.

> *With all the love I can have*
> *for a wonderful woman as you,*
> *John*

"John," the author of the typed note, was John Carlin III, one of the two other men, at least that he knew of, who loved his fiancée, Mechele Hughes. Mechele had handwritten her reply on that same note to Carlin:

Great—
Please don't let anyone know where I am at. But you already know that. ☺ When will the generator be rebuilt and the back door does it close now? I don't mind you going out there. You paid 4 it! Silly! I will clean it up nice don't worry about having it cleaned— love you and Thanks again!

> *Mechele*

She was hiding from him . . . him! The one man who loved her more than any other in the world, more than John

Carlin III, more than her other "love," Scott Hilke, more than anyone! She *must* have known how much that would hurt him. The note had been carefully placed on the kitchen table, where Leppink couldn't miss it. Never mind that the note was his death warrant, and he knew it.

"From the moment I met Mechele at the Bush, I fell in love with her," he wrote in an e-mail to a friend.

He had lately begun to see some serious problems with their relationship. She was still fucking these other guys when she shouldn't have been. She also stole from him, which made him even more furious. But he *had* to see their engagement through to the end. It made no difference whom she *liked*, it was whom she *loved* that counted. And that was he. He knew it in his heart. There was no choice, none at all, none whatsoever. As he left the house, note in hand, Kent Leppink grabbed his red jacket.

Questions, questions, Leppink's mind teemed with questions. Where exactly was this cabin in Hope or near Hope? Was she thinking at all about their wedding plans? They remained unanswered. He got on Seward Highway, which wove around the western shore of the Arm, before turning west onto the Kenai Peninsula. The Kenai goes a full 160 miles out into the Pacific Ocean, just directly south of Anchorage. Cook Inlet on the west separates it from the mainland, while on the east Prince William Sound does the same. But this isn't like the Cape.

Where Cape Cod, Massachusetts, has a hotel and gas station every hundred yards—or so it seems—the Kenai was an isolated place, equal in total land mass to that of New York and New Jersey combined. Seven-thousand-foot glacier-covered mountains ran along the peninsula's southeast coast on the Gulf of Alaska. The last time New York and New Jersey saw glaciers like that was a couple of million years ago.

The northwest coast was a combination of marshland and flats, broken up by small lakes. Larger lakes can be found in the peninsula's interior, along with the salmon-rich Kenai River and the Russian River. After about twenty-five miles west out into the desolate interior, the highway suddenly turned north.

Mechele was such a wonderful person. As Leppink's mind wandered obsessively in thought about Hughes, he turned right on the Hope Highway and drove dead north, back toward Turnagain Arm, heading for the old mining town of Hope, and an old miner's shack where, once and for all, he would finally discover the truth.

"Hope." Like most transplants from the Lower 48, Kent Leppink had come to Alaska with lots of it. Like many before him, he saw Alaska as a place where he could reinvent and perhaps redeem himself for past wrongs. Alaska was the last stop on a thirty-six-year odyssey.

A child of privilege, one of three sons born to his father, Kenneth, a grocery store mogul, and his mother, Betsy, he came from the Lower Peninsula of Michigan, from the Grand Rapids suburb of Shelby in the western part of the state. Surrounded by water on all sides except its southern border, which it shares with Ohio and Indiana, Michigan was a great place to be a child. Kent Leppink grew up with a love of the outdoors that turned to hunting when he was a teenager.

"It wasn't the act of shooting the animal that he liked," the oldest brother, Craig, later said. "It was the work he put into it."

But his hunting skills didn't get him his bachelor's degree. Leppink eventually dropped out of Western Michigan University after trying courses in grocery management. His father, Kenneth Leppink, then brought him in as a cashier to the family business—Leppinks Food Centers. With the family having grocery stores in Belding, Howard, Lakeview, Spring Lake, and Stanton, Leppink continued to work as a cashier at one or the other into his twenties. The hope was that he would work his way up in the family business.

Leppink became the archetypal bachelor uncle—free-wheeling and gregarious; his nieces and nephews loved him. Family members would later say that on the surface he was a crotchety sort of guy, a pose that hid a man who engaged his passions. He became a collector who at one time or another was into rugs, sculpture, and wine. Yet even that was a pose that masked the adventurous man who took vacations in Reno, "the biggest small city in the world," where he enjoyed fine Scotch and even finer women. He wasn't some strange "mountain man" who got off more on his stuffed specimens than a really hot woman in front of him with a gorgeous face and a great body. Leppink would call friends from Reno vacations, inevitably with a new girl by his side and some stories to tell.

Then something happened.

His employment in the family business came to an abrupt end circa 1991 when his family discovered, according to court documents, that "he had embezzled a significant sum from the business." The family refrained from pursuing criminal charges but Leppink was required to surrender stock in the [family] company valued at approximately $1.2 million.

While he hadn't been prosecuted, Leppink continued to push his luck. He moved to Tennessee under an even greater cloud of suspicion, "for setting fire to his home in an unsuccessful attempt to refurnish his coffers. The attempt was unsuccessful because the arson was so obvious that the insurance company refused to pay Leppink's claim."

Nevertheless, at a game farm outside Nashville, Leppink learned the necessary skills to become a taxidermist.

For Leppink, taxidermy was a way to indulge his love of hunting and support himself financially. He got really good at opening up the animal to be mounted, scooping out all the organs, eyes, and blood, and replacing them with preservatives and artificial eyes. Moving further into the hunting world, Leppink attended the Safari Club International convention in Las Vegas.

The SCI is the self-described "leader in protecting the freedom to hunt and in promoting wildlife conservation worldwide." Conventions are primarily about marketing and networking, and Leppink was very good at the latter. At the convention, Leppink met Russ Williams. When Leppink explained that he worked in Tennessee as a taxidermist, Williams nicknamed him TT, which Leppink's friends used affectionately thereafter. He even got the letters "TT" tattooed on his body.

A commercial fisherman from Prince William Sound, Alaska, Williams became friends with the likable Leppink, aka TT; they hit it off. In 1993, Williams offered Leppink a job on his tender, the *Togiak*. Leppink accepted. Just as he'd gotten into the hunting world, he got into Alaska's seafaring community.

Leppink became a sailor on Prince William Sound. He learned how to transport fish from point A to point B efficiently enough to make a good profit. Kent Leppink became respected and well-liked by his colleagues. After just a few years working for Williams, Leppink bought the *Togiak* and went into business for himself. Like so many others who came before him, Kent Leppink finally found who he was and what he was supposed to do in life in Alaska.

Working the *Togiak* himself, he became even more successful. It was time for expansion. Just like his father who had started out with one grocery store and grew into a chain, Kent was going to expand and buy a second boat, and if that worked, who knew? The splendiferous catch in Prince William Sound seemed unending.

The road sign up ahead said "Hope." Located on the peninsula's north shore, Hope was a booming gold rush city long before the 1898 Klondike gold rush. Supplied with the materials in exchange for a promised share of the profits, miner Alexander King rowed a dory up Turnagain Arm in 1888. Two years later, he returned with four pokes of gold. That was enough to get the rush going.

In 1893, eleven miners had staked claims on Resurrection Creek and three on nearby Bear Creek. Then in 1895, five miners extracted $40,000 in gold from the earth. When that news reached Seattle, Turnagain Arm became gold rush fodder. Three thousand people headed to the Arm in 1896. With that many people coming in so fast, it was time to name the place. Hope City got its name when the miners named the town after the next person off the boat—seventeen-year-old prospector Percy Hope.

By the next year, 1897, Hope was overshadowed by the more lucrative Klondike gold rush. Wyatt Earp and other speculators passed through Hope on their way to the riches of the northern gold fields. Murders in Hope were common then, and an accepted way of frontier life. Business picked up when miner Robert Mathison took 385 ounces in less than two months from Resurrection Creek, which runs directly through the town. That brought about ten thousand more people to the Turnagain Arm gold fields.

The creek was lined with prospectors on both sides using cradles to extract the placer gold from the water. Placer gold is gold that has, through erosion, come loose from its host rock where it originated. It was subsequently deposited in a streambed or on a hillside by glacial water or other geological forces. Gold! The Resurrection Creek prosecutors found the shiny stuff embedded in the placer gravels. To get it out, they used a device called a cradle.

Looking like an ordinary baby cradle, it was almost five feet long, constructed out of white pine. It had a headboard, with a hopper at the bottom. Sand and gravel were poured into it, and then water was washed over it. When the cradle is gently rocked back and forth, sand, gravel, and most importantly gold are forced into the cradle's bottom. After that, it was a simple matter to extract the gold. Some was still attached slightly to the host stone to some degree; gold nuggets, small flakes, fine gold, and even down to micron, gold smaller than can be seen with the naked eye.

The turn of the century saw the combines move in with their hydraulic mining equipment, driving the small prospectors out of the Alaska territory. Hope became an almost deserted town, dwindling to a couple dozen hardy souls. By the end of the twentieth century, the town's population had swelled to two hundred, barely surviving on tourist dollars, nostalgia for a bygone era that wasn't so great to begin with. Most prospectors went broke.

Driving through, Leppink could see that placer gold mining out of Resurrection Creek was a long-ago thing. It was just a little creek that flowed north right into the Arm, with nothing to distinguish it except the kind of eerie feeling you get when you go past a cemetery at dusk. The white and green general store on one side of it had been serving customers since 1896. They'll be more than happy to sell you a pan to pan for gold in the creek. Not much left, but you may be able to bring up a few grains.

The social hall, made out of logs in 1902, was still used for life cycle occasions, from confirmations to weddings. The little red schoolhouse, built in 1938, had been turned into a library. The weathered wooden storefronts from another century appealed to gold rush aficionados and other tourists. A little farther north, the town slopes down to the Turnagain Arm tidal flats. On any given day, a tourist could see the endangered American eagle flying over the flats. The four-and-a-half-mile-long Gull Rock follows the cliffs on the south side of Turnagain Arm.

Kent Leppink was oblivious to it all. All he could think about was Mechele. He needed her; he needed to find her. *Now where was the cabin*, he thought. Leppink was hungry and went into a restaurant in Hope. There he struck up a conversation with the cook, Rebecca Douglas.

"I'm looking for my girlfriend," Leppink explained, showing her a picture of him with a very pretty girl. "Have you seen her in town?"

Douglas looked at the photo but came up blank. She'd never seen the woman in her life. After leaving the restaurant, Leppink stopped a few others in town.

"Have you seen this woman?" he asked, showing them the photograph of Mechele and him.

No one had. Kent Leppink got back into his car, drove out of town, and vanished without a trace.

May 2

Chugach electric lineman Jim Hardy parked his truck at mile marker 13.5 of the Hope Road. It was the middle of no place, like much of Alaska. Hardy was on a service call to fix a downed wire out there in the middle of no place. The line was in the woods off the road. He hiked through the brush, looking for the utility pole and the line he was there to repair. Passing a hiking trail, he kept going until he got to the pole.

At first, Jim Hardy thought the guy in the red jacket and blue jeans, who was sprawled on the ground with his hands flung to the side, was just sound asleep. That it was what Raymond Chandler called "the big sleep" did not enter his mind at first. After all, it was a bright, sunny morning. It was not unreasonable to assume that someone had wandered off the isolated hiking trail to take a quick snooze beneath an even more isolated electric company pole in the bush. But as Hardy got closer, he slowly realized that his repair job would have to wait.

The bullet hole through the chest and the one in the cheek were a dead giveaway. The guy in the red jacket was dead. Hardy ran back to his truck to call it in. That was how Detective Preston Wade of the Alaska Department of Public Safety's (DPS) Major Crimes Unit showed up. Unlike similar agencies in many other states, Alaska's DPS is the primary law enforcement and public safety organization for most of Alaska's vast geographic area.

When Alaska entered the Union in 1959, it became the biggest of the United States, easily eclipsing Texas in sheer land area by almost three to one. For the Alaska State Police, that's not such a good thing. There are millions of places in Alaska where you can kill someone, dump the body, and nobody would be the wiser. That's why cops hate body dump jobs, and Wade was no exception.

If the body had been left out exposed to the elements for even a few days where it lay, decomposition would have set in. The more that happened, the more difficult identification would become. It would make matters worse if the killer or killers stripped the body of anything to identify it. But with the guy in the red jacket, Preston Wade caught a break.

From the condition of the body, it looked like the guy had been killed during the previous forty-eight hours. The nights had been cool. It had slowed down the decomp, making it easier to take fingerprints. DNA testing was also possible to establish identity, though it was not as common as it would later become. The coroner would be especially anxious to check the guy's post-mortem lividity.

Lividity, more commonly referred to as livor mortis, begins twenty minutes to three hours after death. During this natural process, blood settles or coagulates in the lower part of the body. This causes a purplish red discoloration of the skin, though this phenomenon does not occur in the area of the body touching the ground. A good coroner can "read" the lividity to approximate the time of death.

Wade noticed that he wore what looked like black Converse sneakers ("Chucks") and that the ankles were crossed. Either he fell that way after he was shot, or someone crossed them for him. Searching the body, he found the victim's car keys. He also pulled a checkbook out of a trouser pocket. Standing, he opened it and read. The checkbook showed an account at the First National Bank of Anchorage in the names of "Kent J. Leppink" and "Mechele K. Hughes."

It was a natural assumption that the decedent was this Kent J. Leppink, unless of course he stole the guy's checkbook, which was also a possibility. Looking further through the pockets of the dead man, once again Wade got lucky. The guy was loaded with stuff. Whoever had pulled the trigger made the crucial mistake of not stripping the body of ID.

From one pocket, Wade took a New York Life "change of beneficiary" form dated April 26, 1996. According to the document, Leppink had changed his beneficiary on a life insurance policy from Mechele Hughes to Kenneth Leppink. With it was a U.S. Post Office receipt dated April 30, 1996 (2:29:08 P.M.).

While the gun caliber and ammunition used had already been established by the shell casings left at the scene, the identity of the killer, or killers, was another matter. So was the exact weapon as well as the motive, though that might become clear after Wade made a few calls back at the office.

Leaving the crime scene technicians to process the scene, Wade hiked back out to where he'd parked his car at mile marker 13.5, got in, and headed back to Anchorage. One thing Wade knew for sure—the killer wasn't a professional. No professional in his right mind would leave identification on a body. While it was nice to rule out a professional hit, they are still the rarity. That just left twenty million other possibilities and more than six hundred thousand suspects.

Back at the office, Preston Wade picked up his phone, listened for the dial tone, and began dialing.

CHAPTER

2

Shelby, Michigan, May 3

Michigan is cold even in May. It's also five hours ahead of Alaska. Shelby is in rural Macomb County, Michigan, a town of seventy-three thousand hardworking residents. It was a Friday, not unlike any other for sixty-two-year-old Kenneth Leppink, but one he would not soon forget. The letter arrived that day in the post.

In April "I had gone to Anchorage to assist Kent in filing his Federal taxes," Kenneth Leppink stated.

He also planned to meet with Kent's fiancée, Mechele, to discuss wedding plans. But things didn't go as planned. When Kenneth Leppink arrived, Mechele Hughes was noplace to be seen, out of town someplace. Kenneth Leppink subsequently left the forty-ninth state on April 30, 1996, returning to his home in Shelby, Michigan. He took his doubts with him. While Kent clearly loved Mechele, it wasn't entirely clear how much she reciprocated.

After returning home, Kenneth Leppink and his wife, Betsy, received the express mail package from their son Kent that contained the two letters. The April 30 date on the receipt meant Kent had sent it shortly after he saw his father off at the airport, for what he obviously suspected would be the last time.

"Kent mailed two letters to his mother and me, one inside the other," Leppink explained. "The first warned of something awful to come, and if I had reason to believe he was dead, to open the second letter, but only upon his death. At 4:30 or 5 o'clock, my son, my other son in Lakeview [Craig] came to let us know that Kent had been shot and was dead. He had been notified by the local sheriff's department."

It was the Montcalm County Sheriff's Office that notified Craig Leppink of his brother's death. It had been easy for Wade to track Kent Leppink's next-of-kin down to Lakeview and Shelby, Michigan.

"It was a tough time," Kenneth Leppink says simply.

Tough or not, Kenneth Leppink was not going to have time to grieve for his son. Kent had told his father that if he "had reason to believe I'm dead," to open the second letter. Murder certainly qualified, and Kenneth Leppink didn't hesitate. Taking the envelope in hands that had once stocked store shelves until he could afford to get someone else to do it, the same hands that signed the documents establishing Leppinks Food Centers, he now had the dubious distinction of opening what could amount to his son's last will and testament.

Most of all, they were hands that had once touched his baby son Kent's head gently. He was about to have the unique experience of reading his baby son's words from beyond the grave.

"I opened the second envelope. After reading it, I called detectives in Anchorage. I faxed them a copy, and then later sent them the original."

Here's part of the text of the note that Kenneth Leppink faxed to Preston Wade:

Since you're reading this, you assume that I'm dead. Don't dwell on that. It was my time, and there is nothing that can change that. There are a few things that I would like you to do for me though I hate to be vindictive in my death, but paybacks are hell.

First of all, pay all my debt with the insurance money. That I owe you. Then go on a nice vacation . . . act like I am there with you and do the things I would like to do. Lie on the beach, fish, relax. 2 weeks minimum but not much longer.

Gary Brooks would like to own the Togiak. Give it to him if you can, otherwise, sell it to him so that he can afford it. Owning the boat might make a difference in his life. . . .

Use the information enclosed to take Mechele DOWN. Make sure she is prosecuted:

—Fraud—She took me for a lot of money on the impression we were getting married. This may be hard to prove without me present, but give it a shot. It is a class B felony in Alaska. $15,000 can be proved because you sent it to us.

—Insurance fraud . . . have the IRS audit her. Turn her in! . . .

—False driver's license and passport . . .

Mechele, John, or Scott were the people, or persons that probably killed me. Make sure they get burned. . . .

Sorry about giving you all this stuff to do. I would have done it, but I wanted to make things work. I wanted to marry Mechele. If that would have happened, this would have all been destroyed. I have kept it as my "insurance policy." Use it! I'll rest easier.

Do me another favor. Make sure Mechele goes to jail for a long time, but visit her there. Tell her how much I really did (do) love her. Tell her you love her, and help her. She has a split personality and the part I fell in love with is very beautiful. I really did want to marry her and make her dreams come true.

Love ya,
Kent

The letter gave contact information for Mechele Hughes, John Carlin III, and Scott Hilke. Kenneth Leppink knew exactly who "Mechele," "John," and "Scott" were. Kent had just named his presumptive fiancée, Mechele Hughes, and Kent's Alaska friends John Carlin III and Scott Hilke as the prime suspects in his murder.

Reading the faxed letter in Anchorage, it was easy for Wade to deduce Kent Leppink was not as much of a sap as some people thought. He had known that his life was in imminent danger, that death was close. He had taken specific precautions to get justice afterward by naming the people he thought were his murderers.

Looked at in that context, his last letter to his parents became, in effect, a suicide note, a confession that the woman he loved more than any other in the world had in some way helped bring about his death, as well as a testament to his love for friends and family.

Every cop knows that most homicides are committed by people who know the people they kill. That's why most homicides are solved and so-called cold cases are few. While Leppink's letter was a stunner, it wasn't a total surprise that the prime suspect Leppink named was his fiancée, Mechele

Hughes. But now it appeared that she also had some sort of romantic relationship with Scott Hilke.

That left the third suspect, John Carlin III. How did Carlin fit in? If Leppink was killed out in the bush, how did his car wind up back in front of his house? Who drove it back? If the killer drove the car back from the murder scene, why did he leave an incriminating note like that? Maybe the killer's subconscious guilt accounted for leaving the clues to his identity, something that clearly would have occurred to any Freudian.

"Mr. Leppink," Wade said over the phone to Kenneth Leppink, "I need to get some more background on your son and his relationships. When did Kent come to Alaska?"

"Kent came to Alaska three or four years ago," Kenneth began. "He came with the idea he was going to work for Russ and Shirley Williams on their fishing business. He started his program with them and all of a sudden Russ has a tender boat and there was a job opening."

A tender boat ferries the catch from the fishing boats to the fish processors.

"That first year, Kent worked on the tender boat as a deckhand. The second year he worked the same way with Russ, only his responsibilities became better and greater. All good things. Last year, Kent bought a tender boat from Russ Williams. He operated it about half the season. This year he was anticipating the fishing business again and he was all anxious to get going."

"Real fast before we proceed any further, you said he was here about three to four years so he arrived in '91 or '92?"

"Something like that, yes."

"And did he drive up or fly up?"

Why not sail up for that matter? The cruise business was one of the things that gave Alaska some of its significant revenue.

"He drove up," Kenneth answered, which meant he took the Trans-Canada Highway.

"And how did he happen to know Russ and Shirley Williams?"

"They met through the Safari Club International. They talked about salmon fishing and Russ offered him a job. He also stayed at Russ's home in Chugiak and he also house sat for them in the wintertime when the fishing wasn't on."

"Okay, what kind of folks are they?"

You could almost see Kenneth Leppink smile through the phone wire.

"They're super people. We stayed there while Kent was living there. They opened their house to us. You'd think it was a Holiday Inn the way they treated us. I have a lot of admiration for both those people."

Which, of course, wouldn't take them off the suspects list in any murder. Everybody is a suspect until ruled out, but the signs immediately pointed to their innocence.

"Do you have any idea or not whether Kent ever had any problems with Russell himself, either when he was employed by him or maybe when he bought this boat and started going into business for himself?"

Remember the one FBI statistic that is unquestioned and still valid (your tax dollars at work): more than 70 percent of homicides are committed by people close to the decedent.

"I have talked with Russ. From what I understand there was a little dissension. With regards to the half year insurance, they buy insurance for a whole season."

There it was again; insurance money. It kept running through the case. Another fight over insurance money. There had also been a "little bit of dissension" over the gas bill. Fuel cost for fishing boats was high in 1996 and continuing to climb.

"Did the dispute between him and Russ involve obtaining attorneys?"

"Kent used an attorney when he purchased the boat. I don't think he acquired an attorney specifically for this situation."

"Did they ever have any arguments over the boat situation?"

Kenneth couldn't recall any. In fact, "They treated him super." He repeated the superlative. "I'm going to call them because I want them to know that there's been a problem."

That was one way to put it. Another was that a very good friend of yours had just been shot and killed. At that moment, at least one person, perhaps more, had gotten away with murder.

"Do you know Kent's girlfriend and can you remember when he first met her?"

"I've only met her one time. Last July in Anchorage. That would have been July 1995. We had a family dinner in Anchorage. That's the only place we met her."

She had also failed to show, as he had said before, when he visited Kent in Anchorage in April.

"And do you happen to know how Kent first met Mechele?"

"He met her at the Bush Company. That's all I know."

"For the purposes of clarification here, you're referring to the Bush Company, a topless dancing joint in Anchorage, is that correct?"

"It's, well, a dancing joint, I don't know is it topless?"

Is the Pope Catholic?

"Yes," Wade answered, to which Kenneth replied, "Okay, you know better than I do."

Well, the place, and earlier places, did have sort of a checkered history and unique place in Alaska folklore. Back to business.

"How much do you know of Mechele's background, of things she was doing before she met Kent?"

"I never had an opportunity to sit down and communicate with Mechele. To be really honest with you, she tried to avoid me. There were several times we were supposed to communicate. They were gonna get married. And every time we were ready to communicate, Mechele couldn't make it. Or wouldn't make it, whatever . . ."

Indeed. Kenneth Leppink of course was heavily implying that Hughes wouldn't communicate with him for a reason. Maybe she sensed his suspicions about the union. After establishing that Kenneth Leppink had been in Anchorage to see his son from April 26, 1996, until he flew back to Michigan on April 30, Wade asked him specifically what the purpose of his visit was.

"There were two reasons," Kenneth answered. "The one was we needed to have some dates. They were gonna be married in our town here in Michigan [Shelby] and we needed to tie down some dates and some places and some things here with regards to their wedding. And the other thing was that Kent was finishing his 1995 income tax returns and he needed some help with that."

"When you were here trying to arrange his wedding and to do his taxes, did he relate any concerns to you about personal problems he may have had with Mechele or other folks here that were associated with him in Anchorage?"

He meant the greater Anchorage area, including Wasilla.

"Yeah, uh hum," Kenneth affirmed reluctantly.

"What did he tell you about that?" Wade pressed.

"He wasn't happy being the fiancé of a girl having other people understand more about where his fiancée was located and what things were going on. He was not informed. Mechele communicated with John Carlin, probably more than she communicated with Kent while I was here."

That would make sense of course if two people were engaging in a conspiracy to murder a third.

"Now, Kent has a computer, and it's important that you find that computer." Kenneth related how he thought there might be "some correspondence in that computer between Mechele and other men?"

He said, "There is a memory on that computer and I think it would behoove you to find that computer and to have somebody that understands computers have those [e-mail] messages brought back up and read off or printed."

Now that would be *direct evidence*!

"So it was definitely your understanding from talking to Kent that he had concerns or suspicions that she been seeing other men?"

"Yes, but through all this, I asked him the question quite pointed, 'Are you intending to marry Mechele, are you gonna reconcile this, ah, situation you have with you and John or with Mechele and John? Is that a reconcilable thing?' And he said, 'I hope so.'"

Hope. Kent Leppink and hope. That seemed to characterize his life, especially when he moved to Alaska.

"How did Mechele feel toward Kent?" Wade wondered. "You think in her own way, she did love him, or was she utilizing him for some other purpose?"

"You asking my opinion?" Kenneth replied.

"Yes," the cop answered firmly.

"I think that Mechele intentionally used Kent," the grocery store mogul answered just as firmly. "I don't know for what because Kent didn't have any money to speak of."

He was actually worth more dead than alive.

"I think she intentionally used him," Kenneth continued, "and abused him."

"How was Kent with women, I mean was he able to get girlfriends or dates pretty easily?"

"No, I don't think so," Kent's father answered.

"So this relationship with Mechele—"

"I don't think all the time he had a relationship with Mechele. He never had another date. It was a super important thing."

"Have you met John Carlin?"

"Yes, I have."

"When was that?"

"While I was up there on the twenty-sixth, that night, John wanted me to stay at their house. I told him that Kent and I had several things we wanted to discuss with regards to taxes and other business and really that I would rather go to a motel or hotel or whatever. We stayed at the Best Western."

"Do you know how many people were at the house that Kent was living at here in Anchorage?"

"Well, there would be just John and his son John."

Wade looked at some notes. He remembered one of the other detectives on the case developing a lead regarding the living arrangements of the suspects.

"Now they had been living in this house in Anchorage while remodeling their house in Wasilla?"

"Yes."

"Do you know what kind of a relationship that John and Kent had?"

"I think they had what I want to say was a 'speakable relationship.' There was no problem as far as I could see. They talked to each other."

So do most victims and their murderers.

"Every time I called up there and if John answered the phone, he didn't cause any problems with regards to getting Kent on the phone. I didn't foresee a super problem there."

Kenneth Leppink didn't have X-ray vision. Even if he had, it wouldn't have done any good—John Carlin was made of lead, impenetrable to X-rays.

"Do you happen to know about handguns or rifles that Kent owns?"

"He used to have this .270 rifle back when he was in Lakeview. Whatever else he's got, I don't know."

"What about Kent's financial situation?"

Wade was closing in on the motive.

"He just bought this boat for $135,000. I loaned Kent $35,000, a personal loan. Then I cosigned his note for the boat for a hundred thousand dollars." Kent had called his father, finally, for help. "He said, 'Dad, I've got a problem with regards to the startup money,'" and his father had done the right thing and helped him.

Then Wade turned to the meat of the case.

"What about insurance policies Kent may have had? Are you familiar with any of those and who the beneficiaries might be?"

"Yes, I am. When we arrived on the twenty-sixth, that night he handed me an envelope. He said, 'I want you to have this.' And I opened it and looked it over and it was a change in beneficiary. It just told me what the policy number was on the policy, its title, Kent's name, and the change in beneficiary. The first beneficiary was me. The second was Betsy, my wife, his mother. The third beneficiary would have been Ransom, his second brother."

"You happen to know who obtained this policy on Kent?" Wade asked casually.

"Kent mentioned that Mechele had bought that policy. For a million dollars."

"Was Mechele aware she would no longer be a beneficiary on that?"

"I don't know how she could have known that."

"So you wouldn't know if Kent spoke to Mechele about it?"

"Not that I know of."

Good. If Hughes had killed Leppink, the motive of a $1 million life insurance policy was readily establishing itself. Kenneth went on to mention something else: that there were some other relevant documents, including a driver's license.

"I have a driver's license and a passport from New Jersey. They don't look alike."

He said they were Mechelle's. However they looked, they showed a trail in Hughes's life back to the Garden State in the Lower 48.

"You happen to know when John Carlin met Mechele?"

"His wife died about a year ago. This is what he told me. Then somebody took him down to the—what's the name?"

"The Bush Company."

"The Bush Company," Kenneth repeated like a mantra, "where he met Mechele."

"What kind of lifestyle do you think Mechele is accustomed to, or seems to like?"

"She knows how to spend money," the grocer answered firmly. "She goes on several trips all over the country. She seems like everything that she has done in this [Wasilla] house you can just see the dollar signs."

More possible motive, and Wade bored in.

"Was the house in Wasilla, did it belong specifically to Mechele?"

"I really can't tell you. I think it belongs to Mechele. But I don't know that. I have a receipt here for $15,000 that Kent put it into the house. I'd send you a copy of that too."

There's a time in every interview where the investigator can sense the person being interviewed is being worn down. With a cooperative witness like Kenneth Leppink, he can always be reinterviewed and probably would be. But the last thing Wade wanted to do was to get into the arcane now.

"Ken, who in your opinion, based on what little you know so far, might have wanted to do something like this to Kent?"

"My first train of thought would be Mechele. My second train of thought would be John Carlin. And my third train of thought would be Scott Hilke, H-I-L-K-E. I say that simply because these are men that Mechele, being the fiancée of Kent's, that she was in communication with."

"Okay, anything else that you can think to add at this time, Ken, that might be important . . ."

"No, I can't think of anything right off the bat. Can you tell me, I have May 2 down as the day they found Kent?"

"Yes."

"Can you tell me what day he died?"

The father looking for definite closure with his son. And a little comfort.

"I can tell you that he appeared not to have been there very, very long," the cop replied gently. "From experience and in what we were able to observe, it didn't appear much over a day, if that long."

"Okay, all right. Just wondering."

"Okay, let me go ahead and end the formal interview for right now, Ken, It's about 12:27 P.M."

Preston Wade turned the tape off, conversed with Kenneth Leppink for a few minutes, and then turned it back on. He had just discovered a reversal.

"Back on tape," said Wade, "at 12:31 P.M. For just a moment. When we were off the line Ken, you had something else you wanted to share with me?"

"Kent went to the town of Hope looking for Mechele because John Carlin owns a cabin or a cottage or something there. He [John] had mentioned that's where Mechele went is to Hope. Kent's first trip down there, he could not find her. I'm assuming that may be where he was headed at [that] point in time."

Carlin had told the father of the man he and Hughes were perhaps plotting to kill that his cabin at Hope was where his son had gone seeking his fiancée. As for Carlin, he claimed to have stayed in town while Leppink went motoring out. If Carlin was the shooter, he was setting up his alibi nicely.

"Does John Carlin [really] have a cabin in that Hope area?"

Kenneth Leppink hesitated.

"I don't know. I didn't see the cabin. But that's what was told to Kent."

"Sounds to me that Mechele may have been down there on some liaison with John. And Kent was looking for her."

"That could be."

"Okay, we'll be off record again with Ken at about 12:33 P.M."

In those extra two minutes of tape, Kenneth Leppink confirmed what was shaping up as a murder plot that had worked. His son was dead. It was looking more and more like two people, Hughes and Carlin, were involved.

Perhaps it was time to talk to Mechele Hughes.

Anyone who has ever thought of going to Alaska for any reason owes a real debt to William H. Seward.

A native of Florida, New York, Seward was an attorney. Joining the Whig Party in the 1840s, he served one term each as state senator and governor of New York State. During this time, he first showed the kind of vision that would become so important to the Union in his later career. Increased spending on education and prison reform were cornerstones of his political philosophy.

Serving from 1848 to 1860 as one of the two U.S. senators from New York, Seward became the leader of the anti-slavery wing of the Whig Party. He hated the Fugitive Slave Act that forced escaped slaves to be returned to their masters. So he put his money where his mouth was, defending runaway slaves in court. His vision came forward once again in 1850 during a speech in which he said that if America didn't abolish slavery, there was going to be a civil war.

When Abraham Lincoln won the nomination for president in the fall of 1860, Seward, who had had designs on the office, gave the "Man from the West" his loyal support. Once again putting his money where his mouth was, in the autumn of 1860 Seward conducted an extended speaking campaign in the western United States, extolling Lincoln's virtues. It was therefore no great surprise that when Lincoln won the election in November 1860, one of his first acts as president-elect was to offer Seward the office of secretary of state. A patriot, Seward accepted.

During the Civil War, Seward extended the province of his office to include a government program to arrest Northerners who supported the Confederacy. Maybe it was because he was such an opponent of slavery and that he finally had the power to do something about it. Seward became hated in the South for the way he used force, intimidation, and possible suspension of constitutional rights to deal with Confederate sympathizers.

More in keeping with his office, Seward confounded the Confederacy again by making it crystal clear to the French and British governments that the United States would not tolerate any support of the Southern upstarts who were guilty of the Federal crime of secession. In April 1864, he argued forcefully in a speech that peace negotiations with the South would have as a working framework "that slavery will be abolished and all slaves must be made unconditionally free."

That did it. It was at this point that Alaska was in jeopardy of perhaps forever being a Russian possession. Seward had proven such a staunch and hated enemy of the Confederacy that John Wilkes Booth included him in his nefarious murder plot to assassinate the president, vice president, and secretary of state in one night in order to destroy the executive branch of the Federal government.

Booth assigned the task of killing Seward to the real killer on his team, Lewis Powell, aka Lewis Paine. In both his identities he was a sociopathic Confederate operative. Almost at the same moment Booth cowardly shot into Lincoln's head from behind at Ford's Theater, blocks away Paine was trying to slit the throat of an already injured Seward. He had had a carriage accident and his neck had been put in a leather brace. Paine's Bowie knife set up sparks when it tried to slice through the tough leather. Undaunted, Paine slashed Seward's cheek to the jawbone before escaping.

Not for long. Twenty-four hours later, he was in custody. The Federal government later stretched Paine's neck, while Seward recovered from his wounds and continued to serve President Andrew Johnson in the same capacity as he had Mr. Lincoln. While many of Seward's critics mocked the purchase of Alaska on March 30, 1867, as "Seward's Folly," and Andrew Johnson's "Polar Bear Garden," Seward knew better.

Alaska had unlimited natural resources and direct access to the Pacific Ocean, which could make it a major port. It was Seward who negotiated the acquisition of Alaska from Russia and got the nation a really good deal. For $7.2 million, the United States bought Russia out of a stake in America at the bargain price of two cents an acre. It would take time before Americans saw it for the brilliant deal it was.

Seward died a few years later in 1872 at the age of seventy-one. Alaska has lots of places named for him, including a prison. The big city in the state, Anchorage, was established pretty late in the state's history as a U.S. territory. Across the Arm, Hope was already eighteen years old when Anchorage was established in 1914. Located off Cook Inlet with easy access to the Pacific and trading with the Lower 48 and Asia, Anchorage became a railroad construction port for the Alaska Railroad.

At first, like most cities in Alaska, it was composed of tents until more permanent structures could be constructed. But it was in the decades from 1930 to 1960 that Anchorage expanded significantly due to the building of Merrill Field in 1930, and Anchorage International Airport in 1951. The Feds of course moved in and established Elmendorf Air Force Base and Fort Richardson in the 1940s.

In 1968 when oil was discovered in Prudhoe Bay, Alaska saw the greatest boom to its economy, and Anchorage, in turn, its greatest growth. Then in 1975 Anchorage did something that New York did a century earlier. It merged with its surrounding communities, in this case Eagle River, Girdwood, and Glen Alps, instead of Brooklyn, Queens, the Bronx, and Staten Island. The new entity became known as the Municipality of Anchorage.

Just as it had a century earlier, Alaska continued to grow in the 1980s. It became known as the place to once again reinvent yourself, the last frontier, the end of the American West, pick your metaphor, but above all else, a place to seek your fortune in so many different ways.

Fortune, of course, can strike in places other than oil wells, like Fifth Avenue across from the Sheraton in downtown Anchorage. At that location in the 1970s, a couple of entrepreneurs established the Great Alaskan Bush Company. It was one of many strip clubs. The Wild Wild Cherry, Arctic Trap, and Booby Trap were its principal competitors. Young women like Mechele Hughes were lured there by the promise of making huge money dancing at one of the burgeoning Anchorage strip clubs.

The first Bush won out. It was so successful that a second Bush opened on East International Airport Road. The second location became even more lucrative than the first, so lucrative that the state moved in to shut them down in late 1985.

Whether the girls are gyrating around the poles, doing their lap dances, or taking their clients back to the shadows where they give them more, the same product is being sold. Strip clubs sell *sex*, and not everyone likes that. They exist on the margins of society. In most places, that is also literal. The second Bush, for example, was set up in an industrial area away from families.

Sometimes in these situations, the line between the sexual entertainment the dancers generally offer and prostitution gets crossed. Stripping is legal; prostitution isn't. Strip clubs can also attract drug dealers, gamblers, and strong-arm guys looking for a piece of the action by providing "protection." There were rumors that Seattle mob boss Frank Colacurio had a piece of the action of the Anchorage strip clubs.

With the right payoffs, certain cops and legislators will generally look the other way and allow the club to operate. If not, anything could happen. When the state suddenly dropped its formidable weight on the Bush, it claimed that the place was indulging in one of the oldest cons in the book: the dancers were seducing customers into ordering expensive drinks, and then taking a cut on the back end.

Big surprise there, stripper pumping "clients" for drinks. That was the whole idea, of course. Anything to make money off the suckers . . . uh . . . customers. During the few weeks the Bush was shut down, the Anchorage cops checked their records and found that during 1985, they had been called sixty-five times to one Bush or the other. That made sense. Sex, topless strippers, men, booze, money, a lot of potential trouble. The Alaska State Assembly revoked the Bush's liquor licenses.

"I think we're classy and we try to run a clean place," Bush Company owner Edna Cox told the *Anchorage Daily News*.

Unfortunately, not everyone saw things Ms. Cox's way. When the Bush had thoughts of further expansion of its stripping ways into the more conservative community of Wasilla, where Leppink would wind up living with Hughes, the city council there passed an ordinance that effectively banned strip clubs within its environs. It looked like the reformers were closing in on the Bush.

By 1989, the first Bush across from the Sheraton was running into problems attracting clientele, as well as basic problems with the facility's maintenance. It shut down indefinitely for repairs and then announced its permanent closing on December 4, 1989. A wistful bit of Alaskan cultural history had just been shaved off the map. That left the Bush II to carry on the tradition.

On May 22, 1990, the Anchorage Assembly's ad hoc committee investigating the Bush on East International Road stopped by for a field visit. Two assemblymen publicly reported that the strippers who were nearly naked—another big surprise—were operating too close to the customers. It wasn't quite clear why this was so bad. That was the whole idea, wasn't it?

Nevertheless, the Alcoholic Beverage Control Board suspended the liquor license of the remaining Bush. The doors of its East International Airport Road location were shuttered for sixty days. As if to make the point that the state didn't really cotton to strip clubs, the first Bush in downtown Anchorage, despite its continued indefinite shutdown, got a sixty-day liquor license suspension too.

Forget about downtown; it was all over there. But the more upscale Bush spinoff on International Airport Road continued to pack them in. Sixty-one days later, it was back in business. East International Airport Road in Anchorage was a run-down four-lane strip of asphalt, dotted with low-lying concrete block buildings, factories, and various commercial businesses. Amid this ugly urban clutter was an oasis of sex.

At first glance, Kent Leppink might have thought that it didn't look like much. There was a metal guardrail at the curb. To the left, brightly marked orange and white barrels blocking off that entrance to the parking lot that completely surrounded the little building on all sides. Next door were two mom-and-pop stores, separated from the Bush property by a wire fence. On the other side was a parking lot, set below street level; no separation fence was therefore needed.

The surviving Great Alaskan Bush Company had a building front that looked like something off the Western Street on the Warner Bros. back lot. It had a weathered, rust painted front, with the entrance/exit right in the middle with two side doors. There were two floors, a roof on either side under windows. The place looked like the whorehouse in *Butch Cassidy and the Sundance Kid*. You could just see Butch and the Kid dropping down from the windows, fleeing across the roof, the "super posse" in hot pursuit

The state's top strip club, the Great Alaskan Bush Company was *the* place where a stripper who knew how to work the men and the pole could make a lot money in a short period of time. In the early 1990s. Bobbi Jo was the star attraction. She was so *good*; guys opened their wallets just looking at her.

It wasn't so much her body. She had high 34C breasts on top of the kind of rib cage that made them look even bigger. A miniscule waist and small, almost boyish hips led down to the kind of dancer's legs that could wrap around a man and make him do whatever she wanted. With all that going for her below the neck, it was what was above it that set Bobbi Jo apart.

Bobbi Jo had a seductive, "Betty Boop" kind of voice, and

the kind of dark eyes that immediately latched on to yours as if to say, "You're mine!" They had depths upon depths, and then as if to complete the whole seductive package, Bobbi Jo had a private, cruel smile. She was in control without saying a thing. In Hollywood, they call it star quality, the ability of a movie star—not an actor—to make you watch the screen regardless of what he is doing. The camera is just kind to him; that's what makes him a star.

Kent Leppink first walked through the front door of the Great Alaskan Bush Company to celebrate a friend's birthday in October 1994. He had finally gotten his life together after a lot of years working at it. When he came through on the other side, he found the girl of his dreams. It was a genuine through-the-looking-glass moment.

When he saw Bobbi Jo floating down the stairs, he was immediately struck by her seductive gaze and that cruel smile. And the body helped. Oh, did it help. In Bobbi Jo's business, being a star meant working a top strip club for top money. Bobbi Jo was the star attraction at the Great Alaskan Bush Company.

Men just opened up their wallets like she had their personal keys. When Kent Leppink walked out of the Bush that night in 1994, he knew that he had found the love of his life. Two years later, when Preston Wade walked deliberately into the place, he noticed that the low-hanging Alaskan sky and the mountains framing the famous club of pleasures made the scene even more bizarre. The sky surrounded everything, seeming to push everything down, especially people.

When he came to investigate, Preston Wade was told by one of the topless dancers—he was having a hard time concentrating—that Bobbi Jo was over at the house she shared in Wasilla with Kent Leppink. John Carlin had gone along with her. Wade also found out that as with all stars, Bobbi Jo was a stage name.

For example, Barbara Stanwyck, the Hollywood star who played the deceitful wife who kills her husband for insurance money in *Double Indemnity* (1944)—her real name was Ruby Stevens. Same with Bobbi Jo.

Her real name was Mechele Hughes.

May 3

It really wasn't hard, just a left and a right, driving over to Wasilla, where Detective Preston Wade found stripper Mechele Hughes and housemate John Carlin III at the house Hughes and Leppink had shared before the couple moved in with Carlin and his son in nearby Anchorage.

"I'm investigating the death of Kent Leppink," Wade explained.

It was the first time anyone from the police force officially informed them of their friend's murder. Wade's manner was nonchalant, watching Mechele Hughes and John Carlin III for any discernable reaction. Wade worked alone; he didn't have a partner. Faced with two people to interview, he did what any good cop would: he separated them and interviewed them separately.

Mechele Hughes went first. He decided to take a low-key approach in interviewing her. Most good homicide cops do that with the prime suspect. You can always put on pressure. Start low-key. Murderers are like anyone else—they usually respond better to a gentler approach.

As the cop and the stripper began talking about her fiancé's death, the faucets opened up.

"What was Kent like?" Wade got in between Hughes's sobbing.

"He was very sneaky. He liked to keep people's social security numbers. In his briefcase, in his pocket, he goes through everybody's mail at the house," Hughes answered in her breathy, quivering voice.

The sobbing continued.

Hughes didn't know that Leppink had named her as the number one suspect, and Wade wasn't going to tell her, at least not yet. He had an advantage that cops rarely get—he was one step ahead of his prime suspect. Now, giving Hughes the benefit of the doubt, people respond to grief in all kinds of ways, and none is the "right way."

But Wade would have to be an even bigger moron than Conan Doyle's Inspector Lestrade if he didn't immediately wonder why the stripper was speaking so ill of her recently deceased fiancé. It sounded as if she really didn't like the guy. Then why marry him? The question hung in the air between them. But Wade didn't voice it; too antagonistic. As his conversation with Hughes progressed, he found out what "at the house" meant.

Leppink and Hughes had shared a home in Wasilla, the Anchorage suburb that had voted to stop the Bush from expanding out into their vicinity. Running for mayor of Wasilla at that very moment was Councilwoman Sarah Palin, who would later go on to be the state's governor and unsuccessful Republican candidate for vice president in 2008. Palin was just as much against the Bush expanding into her neck of the woods as anyone else. But if the strippers wanted to buy property in the town, that was another matter.

Wasilla was more than happy to take their money, hard-earned from their physically demanding profession. Unfortunately, the Hughes/Leppink home had a problem with mold. The couple just happened, *just happened*, to move in with John Carlin III, another of Hughes's customers.

"Do you know anyone who would want to kill Kent Leppink?" Wade asked.

He had to ask the question. It was standard operating procedure for any homicide cop.

"No," Hughes replied firmly.

She told Wade that she and Carlin happened to be at the Wasilla house to search through Kent Leppink's belongings. Hughes went even further, readily admitting to searching through Kent Leppink's car that morning for things that might have belonged to them.

That was a curious thing to do, Wade thought, since she hadn't been officially notified of her fiancé's death.

John Carlin III was still waiting in the wings for his interview. There were a few things that needed to be reconciled.

Hughes clearly didn't like the guy she was engaged to marry. The insurance policy gave her motive for the crime. While a good defense attorney would say that there's nothing incriminating about searching a dead guy's things before you know he's dead, the opposite point would be made by the prosecution: the search was done by the killers to remove any traces of their guilt.

This was way far ahead, though, because it was still too early in Wade's investigation to present the prosecutor with anything. What he needed was direct evidence, like a confession. Maybe there was a way to play one off on the other. Hard to say. But having a pair of prime suspects to question was a damn good way to start.

3

Wade had to wonder if Carlin would corroborate that account. Leaving Hughes to her grief, Wade strolled into the other room to speak to the big guy.

John Carlin III was a big beefy guy who looked like a construction worker, which he had been back home in New Jersey before moving to Anchorage. Speaking easily, like he had nothing to hide, Carlin said that he had met Leppink at a dinner party at the residence of Scott Hilke and Mechele Hughes in Wasilla. The immediate implication, Wade realized, was that Hilke was living with her there, and not Leppink.

Carlin claimed that the house they were standing in was damaged by a faulty vapor barrier that caused the walls to rot out, causing extensive mold damage. Mechele then moved into her friend Carlin's place in Anchorage in November 1995. Two months later, in January 1996, Kent Leppink moved in with them.

"I thought Kent was gay," Carlin stated matter-of-factly.

Now *that* was something new! Leppink was gay?

"Did Kent have any enemies?" Wade asked.

It was the standard question to anyone interviewed in a homicide investigation who knew the decedent, though it is not often in real life you get to ask that question so directly of one of two prime suspects.

"I was not aware of Kent having any enemies," Carlin answered.

He also said that Kent had a laptop computer that he carried around.

"When was the last time you saw Kent?" Wade asked.

"The morning of May 1," the suspect answered.

Wade got him to be specific. Carlin told the cop it was sometime between midnight and 2 A.M. on May 1. He remembered that Kent Leppink had been watching television. Carlin went to bed, and when he woke up later in the middle of the night, he noticed that Kent was gone but his car, Carlin claimed, was still at the residence. Further, Kent Leppink was long gone before Mechele returned from an out-of-town trip.

Carlin was loquacious enough to inform the detective that he was the major financial "supporter for the repair of Mechele's house in Wasilla." Further, Carlin said that he was involved in a romantic relationship with Mechele. He had bought her an $11,000 diamond ring to celebrate what they had together.

"What was Kent Leppink like?" Wade asked, jotting in his notebook.

According to Carlin, Kent Leppink was always checking up on Mechele. To get him off Mechele's back, Carlin wrote Mechele a note for Kent to see, implying that she had a cabin in Hope. It was meant as a ruse so Kent would not know that Mechele had left the state and he would quit bothering her. Carlin said the note was authored by both him and Mechele, and that it was left so that Leppink would find it and believe that Hughes was in Hope, Alaska, not Lake Tahoe, Nevada, where she had really gone to be with Scott Hilke.

If Wade was getting this correctly, Carlin was admitting that the note was a fake to lure Leppink away from Anchorage, where he thought Hughes was, to a distant, remote area where he wound up being murdered. Meanwhile, Hughes was partying with her third lover, Scott Hilke, in Tahoe, not to arrive back in town until after the murder was committed.

Was she wearing Carlin's ring in Tahoe? Wade had to wonder. It sounded like an engagement. Yet Carlin didn't seem to think there was anything wrong with giving in to Hughes as he had, both financially and especially emotionally, and then her "making it" with Hilke in Tahoe while he twiddled his thumbs back in Anchorage. As for the other fiancé, Leppink, in Carlin's version of events the fisherman wasn't a lovesick fiancé but some sort of strange gay stalker. The first thing a beat cop sees are "domestics," one seemingly loving person flying at another in a rage, sometimes with a weapon in hand. Later on, detectives see more subtle homicides, planned out, but committed for the same reasons: passion. Passion for money, passion for power, and sometimes, passion for a woman.

What neither suspect failed to explain was why they had not lost any time in searching Kent's belongs. Leppink's body had been discovered only hours before. Hughes and Carlin had begun their search of Leppink's belongings and car before officially being notified by the Alaska State Troopers of their friend's death.

Wade didn't refer to any of that. So far, the pair was talking and had not "lawyered up." It would be nice if that cooperation continued. At the same time, Wade decided to rely on a tried and tested police technique—get the suspect to repeat the same story and try to catch him in a lie.

That was how he happened to interview Hughes the next day at his office, without Carlin being present. She came in voluntarily; there was no warrant for her arrest. This was really the detective's art—getting the suspect to open up and say something incriminating without a lawyer being present, then giving them their "rights," and *then* getting them to say the same thing on tape.

In an interview room, with the same nonjudgmental tone, Wade took her through her relationship with Kent Leppink.

"I met Kent around September of 1994 at the Bush Company, where I worked as an exotic dancer," Mechele Hughes told the detective.

"For how long did you work, at the Bush I mean?" Wade asked.

Hughes said she worked at the Bush from approximately June 1994 until December 1995. She claimed to be engaged to Leppink, but they hadn't been getting along recently. When pressed by Wade to explain what that meant, she tried to make it clear.

"There was no sexual relationship," she said.

She actually suspected that Kent was gay or bisexual. In fact, her boyfriend, she claimed, had not been Carlin but Scott Hilke. He was a traveling salesman from northern California and was up in Anchorage every once in a while. She had met Hilke at the Bush too, and they had become lovers. As for Kent, they had a business together, M&K Enterprises, which was actually the fishing tender *Togiak*.

"Where is it, the boat I mean?" Wade asked.

"I don't know," Mechele answered. "I haven't seen Kent since I got back from Lake Tahoe."

"When was that?'

"May second," Mechele answered.

If Hughes was telling the truth and was out of town the same day the body was discovered, she couldn't have killed him. Or at least that was the way it seemed.

"I had spoken to Kent the night before I came home," the stripper continued. "Kent was supposed to pick me up at Anchorage Airport on the morning of May 2," but had not shown up, which forced her to call John Carlin III for a ride.

Thinking about the .44 Magnum that had been used to kill Leppink—they still had not recovered the murder weapon—Wade turned the conversation toward Hughes's Second Amendment right to bear arms. She admitted to taking a gun class at the Firing Line firing range and using Kent's "big black gun."

"What caliber was it?" Wade asked nonchalantly.

Mechele was unsure, either a .44 Magnum or .45 caliber gun. A few minutes later, the door to the interrogation room opened and in walked Carlin escorted by a state trooper.

"Do you know where Kent's big black gun is?" Hughes asked Carlin.

Unprepared for the question, Carlin hesitated. His uncertain reply was that he was not sure he had ever seen Leppink's gun in the first place.

With the suspects gone, Wade examined the letter again. Leppink wrote:

> *Mechele, John, or Scott were the people, or persons that probably killed me. Make sure they get burned.*

With just a few phone calls and interviews, Wade was able to prove that Leppink had been wrong, at least in the case of Scott Hilke. Hilke was ruled out as a suspect by the simple expedient of having been someplace else during the period Leppink was missing and murdered. That entire time, he was out of Alaska, in northern California. Wade confirmed that through state police sources in California. He also confirmed that Hilke was affianced to Hughes.

As the investigation progressed, Wade and the troopers discovered that the three men who began as Hughes's customers at the Bush—Leppink, Carlin, and Hilke—all had that one little thing in common: they were affianced to Hughes *at the same time*. How much they each knew *exactly* about Hughes's ultimate decision about who she would marry was unclear. In a way, it almost wasn't relevant.

One thing kept nagging at Wade—Leppink's Dodge Omni. It was found, after the body was discovered, parked in front of Carlin's Anchorage home. How had it gotten back to Anchorage, unless someone drove it from the crime scene? Could that mean that two people were actually involved at the scene? Yet Hughes didn't arrive back in town until after the murder.

On his car's front seat was the note that had lured him out to Hope. Kent Leppink had been conned, used as a sap. There simply was no cabin; the cabin didn't exist. The note had clearly been used to lure Kent Leppink into an ambush, where three .44 Magnum slugs tore into his body and killed him.

Wade turned his attention to the third fiancé, named in Leppink's letter to his parents as a suspect in his murder—John Carlin III.

It was the kind of story you read in the *Ladies' Home Journal* but without the upbeat ending.

John Carlin III hailed from Elmer, New Jersey. Only forty-seven miles northwest from the Atlantic City high life, Elmer was rural enough that the "upstaters" from Hoboken and Weehawken thought of it as Redneck County. Carlin's problem was not being thought of as a redneck. He was a married construction worker with a thirteen-year-old child, John IV; and a wife, whom he loved. Carlin was devastated when she developed a fast-acting cancer.

A devoted husband, Carlin listened as his wife expressed a dying wish to see the aurora borealis before she passed. Commonly referred to as the northern lights, the nightly atmospheric phenomenon of multicolored lights is best seen in the polar zone. In 1994 Carlin decided to give his wife her dying wish and moved with her and John IV to Anchorage, Alaska. It was a wonderful thing to do, and Carlin was happy to do it.

When Carlin's wife died—having finally seen the aurora borealis—Carlin was left alone to care for their young son, John Carlin IV. Then fortune smiled. During the 1980s, Carlin had worked on the repair of Philadelphia's Benjamin Franklin Bridge. There was substantial rehabilitation and modernization of the structure that exposed some workers to the damaging effects of the toxic lead paint the bridge had been painted with. Carlin subsequently claimed in a lawsuit brain damage as a result of that exposure. His lawyers had just settled his insurance claim for $1.3 million.

He was ripe. By that time, Carlin had already gone to the Great Alaskan Bush Company. From the delights inside, he chose Mechele Hughes for a lap dance. Something about her just made him fall for her instantly. Mechele seemed to have that effect on guys. The ones who did fall in love with her liked to fete her. Carlin was no different. Carlin was suddenly flush with money. Like many people, Carlin thought it could buy his way out of his grief.

The state troopers' further investigation showed that Carlin gave Hughes a $3,200 fur coat and then, as the ultimate romantic gesture of a guy from New Jersey, an $11,000 diamond ring inside an ice cream sundae! According to all accounts, Hughes took the presents gladly.

Among other things, Wade discovered that while engaged to Leppink, and living with him, Hughes flew to Amsterdam with Carlin, who proposed marriage on Christmas Day, 1995. Hughes accepted. She failed to mention she was already engaged to Leppink and Hilke.

It took three days before the story of Kent Leppink's murder finally hit the local paper that everyone in the Anchorage area read, the *Anchorage Daily News*. Buried on page B5, it merited all of 364 words. That wasn't too surprising. In 1996, Alaska had a murder rate of 7.4 per 100,000 people, exactly the same murder rate as New York City. When murders are that common, they rate little ink, and on an inside page at that.

As for the murder note Leppink left behind naming Mechele Hughes et al. as the prime suspects in his murder, police kept that to themselves. The last thing Wade needed was the dynamic duo reading about their involvement in the homicide in a newspaper piece. That'd make them run. Therefore, no suspects were named in any news story; police did not disclose the contents of the note to the press.

They also did not disclose that except for that note, there was no direct evidence tying Hughes and Carlin III to the homicide. Sure, the note was incriminating, but it only provided the motive for the crime. First-year criminal justice students—and anyone who has ever watched *Law & Order*—know that you also need to prove the means and the opportunity to commit murder before getting a conviction.

And the murder weapon. Boy, it would be helpful to recover it. It was frustrating. Without cause, Wade and the state troopers couldn't get a search warrant for the home Hughes, Leppink, and Carlin shared. Had they been able, the hope would have been to recover the murder weapon and perhaps some other incriminating evidence. Perhaps the autopsy would turn up something that would open up the case.

Kent Leppink's body was laid out on the medical examiner's metal table. Norman Thompson, the state's deputy chief medical examiner, conducted the autopsy.

Thompson carefully noted that the decedent was shot three times, at close range—once in the back, once in the stomach, and once in the face. According to Thompson, powder burns indicated that the gun was either touching Leppink's skin or within inches of it when the first bullet was fired. Because there was little blood transfer from the stomach and back wounds to his T-shirt, a logical assumption would be that the first bullet into his cheek did him in. Establishing time of death was another and more difficult matter.

Noting the body's lividity and the temperature of the organs, Thompson figured Leppink must have been dead a minimum of twelve hours prior to the lineman discovering his body. That would mean Leppink died sometime around 4 A.M. or prior. Thompson had to remain careful of the exact time because the lowering of the temperature during the cool Hope nights had slowed rigor mortis.

The laptop computer arrived on Melissa Williams's Moab, Utah, doorstep unannounced.

She had not been expecting it or the request from her younger sister, Mechele, to erase the files on the hard drive. Melissa was more tech savvy than Mechele and could easily have done the job. Instead, she *refused*. Part of it probably had to do with their personal history.

Mechele Hughes was born in New Orleans, Louisiana, on October 12, 1972. A beautiful child, she was fortunate. Her father was a captain in the air force when the Vietnam War was about to end. The war's end in April 1975 meant a redeployment of forces, her father assigned to another venue. Amazing how history repeats itself, isn't it?

When Mechele was almost twelve, she was diagnosed with scoliosis. That put her in a body brace for nine months, with constant visits to the hospital. Worse, to correct the condition, doctors implanted a steel rod to straighten her spine. Eventually taken out, the rod left a scar from her neck to the small of her back. It did, however, correct her posture, which became absolutely perfect.

From 1986 to 1990, Mechele attended Saint Scholastica Academy in Covington, Louisiana. After a second divorce, her mom, Sandy McWilliams, resettled herself and her daughters, Mechele and Melissa, near New Orleans, where she had relatives and family history. Growing up into a vivacious teenager, Hughes excelled in school, getting A's and B's. Then, at age seventeen, she decided to try her luck in the Big Apple.

She left home a hopeful teenager and wound up moving to New Jersey. There she worked as a deli clerk while doing a second shift as a secretary at a modeling agency, hoping to get modeling work. From there, in some way, she got into stripping.

Well, maybe not quite. That was one version of Hughes's life, the version her mother, Sandy McWilliams, would later tell reporters. As Preston Wade began investigating the mysteries of the Bush, another version of Mechele Hughes's life surfaced.

Mechele Hughes had a great body and a great face, but she also had great ambition. According to police, in 1987, when she was fourteen years old, Hughes took three-year-older sister Melissa's ID and left their New Orleans home. She traveled north, eventually ending up on the Jersey Turnpike and then the Garden State Parkway. On the parkway she traveled to her final stop, Brick Township, Ocean County, New Jersey. There, using her sister's ID, she worked as a stripper in area clubs.

Mechele Hughes honed her stripteasing talents. Hughes left the Garden State at twenty-one and moved to Anchorage to make the big bucks. After Kent Leppink's murder, Melissa Williams would later claim that during her phone conversations with her sister, not only didn't Mechele show any remorse about Leppink's death, she screamed at her over the phone. Melissa's absolute refusal to erase the hard drive, and what apparently were files Mechele was trying to hide, angered Mechele and loosened her tongue.

"It's too bad someone didn't torture him first. He got what he deserved. People didn't like him and he hunted and stuffed animals." Hughes disapproved of hunting and stuffing animals.

When Preston Wade called, Melissa Williams didn't tell him about her incriminating conversations with her sister. But the cop was actually keeping pace. His investigation showed that Mechele had a laptop computer which belonged to Kent, that she had sent immediately after Leppink's death to her sister in Utah.

The cops wanted to see what was on it. Meanwhile, ballistics was also working. Firearms expert Robert Shem from the Alaska State Crime Laboratory examined two bullets recovered during the autopsy of Kent Leppink. The third had not been recovered. Shem looked closely through his microscope at the rifling characteristics of the spent bullets. After he twisted his scope this way and that, the picture became clear.

"It's my opinion that the bullets were fired from a .44 Magnum Desert Eagle semiautomatic pistol," Shem told Wade.

Now that was *very good*. The cops now had a specific murder weapon to search for. Could anyone have seen the gun before it became a murder weapon? Many murderers make the mistake of allowing people around them access to a weapon they will later use in a murder. It's a form of premature bragging, a narcissistic tendency that many criminals have.

Carlin's now seventeen-year-old son, whom the family referred to as J4, was a bit precocious. Investigation showed that he had shown a gun that matched the description of the .44 Desert Eagle to some of his friends before the murder. When questioned, the teen indicated it was his father's gun.

May 7

Rodney Decristofario was the manager of the Firing Line shooting ranges in Anchorage.

"Yeah, there was a dancer in here," he said, responding to Wade's question. "She had a Desert Eagle .44 Magnum that she said belonged to her boyfriend."

"How come you remember this?"

"Because," he said without wavering, "this was the very first Desert Eagle I've ever seen. In my experience, it's an unusual weapon." He was right, and especially in Alaska.

Certain weapons belong in a category of their own because they innovated. Sam Colt's 1836 invention of the first revolver that fired six bullets instead of the one then common to percussion pistols; John Browning's automating of the manual shotgun in 1906, followed up with the tremendous achievement of the Browning Automatic Rifle (BAR); and George Thompson's Model 1928 Thompson submachine gun all belong in this category.

A new addition was the Desert Eagle, conceived in 1979.

According to the Desert Eagle's Website, "when three people with an idea for creating a gas-operated, semi-automatic, Magnum-caliber pistol founded Magnum Research, Inc. in St. Paul, Minnesota." The company patented its unique design for the Desert Eagle in 1980. The first working prototype of the pistol was completed in 1981. But it was still only 80 percent functional, "with a rotating bolt, full gas operation, and excellent shooting characteristics."

That's when the Israeli gunsmiths came in. Israel Military Industries (IMI), under contract to Magnum Research, Inc., handled the other 20 percent that made the gun 100 percent operational. The gun they created is described by Magnum Research as follows:

> Desert Eagle is a gas operated, locked breech weapon that uses stationary (but removable) barrel. Locking is achieved using the separate rotating bolt with four radial lugs that enter the breech of the barrel for engagement with respective cuts. Bolt is inserted into open-topped slide, which is operated using gas, which is bled from the bore through the small port drilled close to the chamber. Short stroke gas piston is located below the barrel closer to the muzzle, and gas chamber is linked to the gas port with long channel, bored below the barrel. Trigger is of single action type, with exposed hammer and ambidextrous safety, located at either side of the slide. Magazines are single stack, with different configuration for each major caliber. Sights are either fixed or adjustable; both front and rear being dovetailed into the barrel and slide respectively. Recently made pistols also had top of the barrel shaped to accept scope rings directly.

Magnum Research took about one thousand fully functional .357 Magnum production models and put them through their paces, test-firing each weapon. Collector's items today, these initial .357 Desert Eagles "have traditional land-and-grove rifling, and they will not accept extended barrels or caliber conversion kits. The serial numbers for these pistols start at #3001." But the Desert Eagle was still not finished innovating. In 1985, the barrel's rifling was changed to increase the Eagle's accuracy. The following year, the company put out a .44 Magnum version of the Eagle. What made it unique was that this "was the very first semi-automatic .44 Magnum pistol successfully brought to market."

By 1989, the Mark VII edition of the Desert Eagle became standard. All Desert Eagle pistols manufactured since 1989 have Mark VII features, including a two-stage trigger, an enlarged slide release, and enlarged safety levers. Then in 1996, Magnum Research, Inc. introduced the .50 caliber Action Express Desert Eagle Pistol. Meant to fill an unmet need in the sporting/hunting market that Kent Leppink so favored, the weapon is capable of bringing down a full-grown grizzly bear with one well-placed shot.

The firing range operator, Rodney Decristofario, had said that "in my experience, it's an unusual weapon." He was right. Produced in small numbers, the Desert Eagle was a rare weapon to find, especially in a distant place like Alaska. If you wanted one, you had to go out of your way to find one.

It was commonly known that the Desert Eagle was used by United States special ops forces. It was a particularly deadly weapon. That's probably what made John Carlin buy the gun.

CHAPTER

4

May 6

Even Preston Wade did not suspect that there was a reason he felt like he was inside a movie. And that made sense. Wade was a homicide detective. His was not a film history background. All he was after was to catch a murderer. That is what led Detective Preston Wade to New York Life Insurance agent Jack Montgomery. Wade found him in his downtown Anchorage office.

"One month before Kent's murder, Kent and Mechele Hughes came in to see me. They arranged for life insurance policies," Montgomery explained in a confident, authoritative voice. "Mechele Hughes was for $150,000, while Kent's was for $1,000,000. Mechele was the beneficiary on Kent's policy and Kent was the beneficiary on Mechele's."

Montgomery consulted his notes.

"Mechele Hughes paid the premiums on both policies using her personal checking account," he stated.

Now a possible motive had become clear. If Mechele Hughes had Kent Leppink killed, she would inherit $1 million. Regardless of the year, 1948, 1996, or 2009, $1 million is a lot of money and more than enough motive for many people to kill.

"Why now," Wade wondered aloud. "Why was Kent getting these policies now?"

"Because Kent and Mechele were getting married."

Montgomery didn't have much more to give him, so Wade concluded the interview. Outside his office, the cops chatted up the New York Life Insurance agent's secretary, Hallie Reynolds.

"The last time I talked to Mechele was on the phone," she said.

Reynolds consulted her phone log.

"It was on April 30. Mechele said that the wedding had been postponed for about two months and the reason was, they were short of cash. Mechele wanted to know if they could get their money back for the policy."

Now that was balls. If the motive for the murder was the insurance policy money, then Hughes was so cheap, she wanted to get the money she had paid for the policy back, even while planning for it to pay off the full million.

"Did either of them, Mechele or Kent, indicate to you that a change of beneficiary form had been filed?"

"No," Reynolds answered firmly.

The next stop was Kent Leppink's personal attorney, Brian Brundin. Wade found him in his office in downtown Anchorage. Rick knew Leppink was dead and was ready to talk. He told the cop that in September 1995, Kent Leppink called and asked for his help in making out a will.

"He told me that until the note on his boat was paid off, the bank and his father would have control over his fishing company. But he wanted Mechele to be his sole beneficiary."

This meant the fishing business, aka the *Togiak*, which was worth more than a million.

"Then on April 19, he came [barging] into my office and told me that Mechele had an affair with a man they were living with last summer while Kent was out fishing."

A later court document would name this person as Scott Hilke.

"Kent and Mechele are living in John Carlin III's house. Kent thought an affair was going on between Mechele and John Carlin and that Carlin was giving Mechele money."

Shortly after, their conversation ended. Kent Leppink returned on April 26. This time he was really upset.

"He said that Mechele had taken him for a $10,000 computer and that things from his storage shed were missing, including a bronze statue and two antique rugs."

He also didn't know where his loving fiancée was.

"Kent said that he had already been to his insurance company and removed Mechele as the beneficiary on his life insurance policy. He asked how he could end the will with Mechele as the beneficiary. I told him, 'The way to end the will is to tear it up.'"

And that's just what Kent Leppink did.

"Kent tore up the will and I threw it in the trash."

"Did you ever do another will for him?" Wade asked.

"No other will was prepared for Kent by me."

A check with Alaska Airlines showed that a ticket was purchased by John Carlin III, using Scott Hilke's credit card, for Mechele Hughes to fly from Anchorage to San Francisco on the same day of the purchase, April 25. Alaska Airlines records show that she departed Anchorage at 3:16 P.M. and returned on May 1.

In interviews with Scott Hilke and others, it was learned that about ten days after Kent Leppink proposed to Mechele Hughes, she finally accepted. Simultaneously, Hilke proposed marriage to Hughes and she accepted. To complicate matters, Carlin proposed marriage around Christmas 1995. Hughes accepted, making Carlin fiancé number three. That made three fiancés, all of whom knew the others existed, but without knowledge that they were all, well, equal.

Sometimes in real life suckers do something to screw up the happily-ever-after. Unknown to Mechele Hughes, even as she allegedly was planning to murder him, Kent Leppink had taken her out of his will as the beneficiary. That was in addition to taking her off as the beneficiary on the life insurance policy, which meant that for sure, positively, absolutely, she could never make a dime on his death.

June 26

There's this line in just about every detective movie ever made probably since *The Maltese Falcon* (1941). In the film, it's Humphrey Bogart's private eye, Sam Spade, who is considered the prime suspect in the murder of his own partner, Miles Archer, who is warned.

"Don't leave town," Ward Bond's detective, Tom Polhaus, tells Spade.

It's a classic, isn't it? In real life, at the first opportunity, the prime suspects hightail it out of town. After all, the key to being a successful criminal is the ability to elude capture at all costs. Do that and no one writes about you, let alone knows you exist.

Does it look suspicious to the cops if you do that? Sure, but it's better than the alternative, isn't it, waiting around for the cops to figure it out and come and *get you*? Heck, Dr. John H. Holliday Jr., aka Doc Holliday, one of the most famous criminals in American history, successfully eluded capture for most of his criminal career for a string of killings. He simply jumped jurisdiction at the first opportunity, sometimes with the help of his old friend Wyatt Earp. You don't need a Ph.D. to figure that one out, though Doc did have a doctor of dentistry.

No, the truth is, jump states and you have a better than even shot of eluding capture. Resources have to be brought to bear to track you, let alone charge you and then extradite you. Put another way, you'd better have something more than just circumstantial evidence to go on for prosecution, because it's gonna cost a heckuva lot of money to get the suspect back from where he has gone to ground.

Real-life suspects who split up obviously have a better shot at avoiding capture. Any police force can marshal only so many resources to bear on a given case at a given moment. By splitting up, any criminal duo gains an advantage because their adversaries have to then split their forces. Not to mention overtime and all the practical things that go into any administrative budget, of which the police are a part.

Sometime in mid-June, 1996, Mechele Hughes left Alaska for the Lower 48, accompanied by the boy she thought of as a her stepson, seventeen-year-old John Carlin IV. She was only six years older than he was. After stopping in California, where she visited Scott Hilke in Sacramento, she turned west and drove toward Utah.

Preston Wade picked up his phone.

"Hello?"

This was before caller ID and you actually didn't know who was on the other end of the line.

"This is Melissa Williams. I'm Mechele Hughes's older sister."

Williams went on to tell the cop that her sister had just left Moab, Utah, after visiting her there for a few days. She wanted to know if Hughes was involved in the murder of

Kent Leppink. She was suspicious because her sister said to her about Kent, "he deserved it," and "too bad he wasn't tortured before he died."

That's when Williams explained that Hughes had sent Leppink's laptop to her on May 6.

"Why?" Wade asked.

Because, Williams answered, Hughes wanted her to clear the laptop of e-mails. She absolutely refused to comply with her younger sister's request. When Mechele left Moab, she took the unerased laptop with her.

"Where's she going?" Wade asked.

"To New Orleans, Louisiana, to visit my and Mechele's mother," she answered.

Their mother's name was Sandy McWilliams. Melissa also gave her mother's address and her place of employment.

"What's she driving?"

"She's pulling a U-Haul behind her motor home," Williams answered.

John Carlin loved Mechele Hughes dearly. He would do anything for her. But money and gifts and things seemed to be what she liked the best. Carlin had gone out and plunked down an $18,000 down payment on a brand-new RV.

Wade ran Hughes's and Carlin's names through the motor vehicle database to get the RV's tag number. The information gathered from his interview with Williams and his other sources made it clear that Mechele Hughes was a very smart woman. Melissa Williams had said during their phone conversation that Mechele had sent the computer to her "the other day" (she couldn't remember which day) to fix because it was not working.

Actually, that was a lie. Mechele had not yet mailed the laptop to her sister. According to the Mail Box Etc. receipt, it was mailed on May 5. Persisting, Wade went back and asked Melissa Hughes, more about the laptop.

* * *

Sergeant Stewart Schwartz of the Louisiana State Police Region 1 Detectives received an alert on his pager to call his lieutenant, Bucky Rogers, commander of Region 1 Detectives. When he did, Rogers told him that the Alaska State Police had requested assistance in locating a suspect in a homicide who was driving a motor home to the New Orleans area.

"Alaska wants us to locate Mechele Hughes and obtain a search warrant to retrieve this Gateway 2000 laptop computer," Rogers explained. "It may contain information relevant to their murder investigation."

Schwartz immediately telephoned Preston Wade.

"What's the mother's address?"

Wade gave it to him. Computers are wonderful tools in police work, but anyone who says they or anything else can substitute for foot leather is more than naïve—he's stupid. Sooner or later, the cop has to go out into the field to get the job done. Schwartz drove out to the mother's residence. It was on Jefferson Avenue in New Orleans Parish. Schwartz didn't stop. He made a few passes in his unmarked car. There was no sign of the motor home, or Hughes for that matter.

Schwartz realized that their best shot was not so much going after Hughes, but the vehicle itself. Back at the office, he got Preston Wade on the phone.

"Give me some more specifics on the RV," Schwartz requested.

Wade gave it to him. Armed with that information, Schwartz immediately turned to Trooper Michael Frey in the intelligence division. Frey ran all of it through the Department of Motor Vehicles computer database. Out popped the information that Mechele Hughes had gone to the office of motor vehicles in Mandeville to obtain a Louisiana driver's license.

"Okay," Schwartz said to Frey. "Let's see if we can locate

Mechele Hughes by searching the motor home parks in the area."

"Good idea, Stew," Frey responded.

It was if it worked. About one-thirty in the morning on July 1, the two cops silently and quietly searched the Fountain Blue State Park in St. Tammany Parish (aka county) between Mandeville to the west and Slidell to the east. It was a great place to picnic, hike trails, and swim in Lake Pontchartrain. It was said that the view from the beach at sunset was among the best in the state. It was also a popular place with campers and RVers alike. The two cops went through the RV section. Their flashlights picked out license plate numbers; not one matched.

They checked the park's daily register of motor homes. Sure enough, Hughes had stayed there in the park over the weekend for two nights and left sometime on June 30. She had left and gone to Riverside State Park. The next day, Schwartz and Frey got back in their cruiser and drove quickly to Fairview, which was also in Tammany Parish. It was about two forty-five in the afternoon when Frey, who was driving— Schwartz had a tendency to get a little excited—spotted the motor home.

"There it is," he said, and pointed through the windshield.

Schwartz saw it parked like any other, the Grand Manor motor home. It had a temporary Alaska tag.

"Drive back out," said Schwartz.

At the gate he flashed his badge at the attendant.

"You check the people in at Lot 66?"

"Uh huh."

"Can you describe them?"

"Sure," and the attendant proceeded to give exact physical descriptions of Mechele Hughes and seventeen-year-old John Carlin IV. "They're paid up until Wednesday."

That was very good; time to get a search warrant.

"Set up surveillance on the motor home," Schwartz told Frey. He didn't need to add that under no circumstances were they to be allowed to leave. Leaving to go to back to headquarters to draft a search warrant he would need to go into the motor home, Schwartz knew the surveillance was in good hands. Frey had been at the top of his class in high school before he joined the force.

At five-thirty, Schwartz returned with the search warrants. Signed by the duty judges of the Twenty-second Judicial District Court of St. Tammany Parish, they included a separate warrant to search the home of Hughes's grandparents in Mandeville for the laptop. The Louisiana cops were doing themselves proud. No stone was going to be left unturned in recovering evidence for their Alaska brethren.

Unfortunately, neither Hughes nor Carlin IV was home. Frey's surveillance had made that clear. Time to wait. Get everything in order, account for all the people in the mobile home. Finally, at ten minutes after 11 o'clock at night, Hughes and Carlin IV returned from a long walk. Lieutenant Bucky Rogers gave the order to move in.

Like two lawmen from the Old West, Schwartz and Frey walked toward the motor home. Spotting them, Mechele Hughes tried to sidle away. As her walk speeded up, so did Schwartz. He took out his badge and held it up.

"I'm a Louisiana State Trooper!"

Hughes was smart enough to stop. Schwartz led her back to the motor home

"I'm a Louisiana State Trooper," Schwartz repeated, and presented her with a copy of the search warrant. Faced with no choice, Hughes had to let Schwartz and Frey in. The first thing Schwartz noticed when he walked in was the laptop computer on the kitchen table. It appeared that someone had been operating it. There were several "how to" diskettes on the table alongside the computer. One that Schwartz picked up was an instructional diskette on "how to boot up a computer."

Schwartz made out a receipt for the computer and diskettes and confiscated them all.

"How'd you come to leave Alaska?" he asked young Carlin.

The teenager replied, "Me and Mechele drove down from Alaska and were to live in a house Mechele was purchasing. My dad, John Carlin, Jr., was going to drive Mechele's jeep down to New Orleans to meet us."

In general terms, he spoke of how he was angry with his father. He wouldn't go into much detail. He explained how he and his father came to be in Alaska, and how his father met Mechele Hughes in the Great Alaskan Bush. The teenager went on to say that he was having personal problems and that he had been suffering bouts of depression.

It had been a couple of long flights from Anchorage to New Orleans. Preston Wade got up from the chair he had been sitting in and shook Stewart Schwartz's outstretched hand when Schwartz came through the door of the police station. The Alaskan cop had gone about as far south as you could in the Lower 48, and was in Louisiana to take his evidence back personally.

"Let me show you around," said Schwartz.

He escorted Wade in an unmarked vehicle out to the location in the Mandeville/Covington area so he could familiarize himself with Mechele Hughes's background. The RV was still there, and Wade thought a little conversation might be in order.

Unfortunately, Mechele Hughes had already left in her RV.

CHAPTER

5

1996–1997

The murder of Kent Leppink would become known in the millennium as the case of the "killer stripper." That was appropriately bizarre because in 1996, just when it seemed that a weird case couldn't get any weirder, Wasilla's mayor, thirty-two-year-old Sarah Palin, got involved.

Or didn't.

Murder doesn't happen in a vacuum. That Wasilla even exists as a place Kent Leppink could have settled in was due to Knik (pronounced "Ken-ick"). Knik was the first boom town in the Matanuska-Susitna Valley, twenty-five air miles northeast of Anchorage. The locals just called the place "the Valley."

By 1915, Knik was a thriving metropolis of five hundred whose job it was to provide for the needs of the men and women in the nearby gold fields of Cache and Willow Creek. Like their brethren before them in the 1848 California gold rush, the miners hoped to haul out pounds of the heavy metal. Just as in California, and every gold rush since, most of them didn't. Common sense notwithstanding, the opportunity to change their lives overnight with a gold strike was enough to keep the people coming to Alaska.

In 1917, Wasilla was established as a stop on the Alaskan Railroad at the intersection of the Knik-Willow mining trail. Because Wasilla had better proximity and access to the gold fields than Knik, Knik moved lock, stock, businesses, and homes to Wasilla. Soon, Knik was a ghost town that faded into Alaska's history.

Wasilla continued to supply the gold miners' needs, but as the twentieth century progressed and the gold dwindled, bio-fuel became very valuable. During World War II, the town supplied the coal miners who had come to the Valley. Also, because it was a major railroad stop, many soldiers passed through on their way to assignment. One of the soldiers who passed through Wasilla during World War II was Samuel Dashiell Hammett. He was on his way south on assignment in the Aleutians. Had they existed, his fictional detectives Sam Spade (*The Maltese Falcon*) and Nick and Nora Charles (*The Thin Man*) would have been much use in Wasilla a few decades hence on the Leppink homicide.

By the end of the twentieth century, the Valley had become a place where huge, some said mutant-size, vegetables and fruits were produced during a growing season that lasted almost a third of the year. A local farmer even set a world record with a 64.8-pound cantaloupe. "It was gorgeous," recalls Adrienne Alper. She was vendor and exhibits manager for the fair where the mutant was exhibited. "It sat on a big table and people were just going over it."

Mutant produce aside, being "the Last Frontier" also meant things happen slower in Alaska. The place didn't become a state until 1959 and Wasilla didn't finally become an incorporated town until 1974, the same year Kent Leppink turned fifteen years old in Michigan.

Eleven years later in 1985, Wasilla voted to ban public nudity in the town's environs. That came about after the Great Alaskan Bush Company, the most notorious strip club in the state, had threatened to expand into the town. With two thriving locations forty-three miles northeast in Anchorage, the Bush had a desire to spread its treasure trail up to Wasilla. But the only treasure the town was interested in was real estate.

The Wasilla town board voted to deny the opportunity to the strippers to practice their exotic talents in town. However, they were more than happy to let Mechele Hughes, and the other exotic dancers at the Bush, purchase homes in the small town of forty-two hundred. It was in Wasilla that Mechele Hughes settled, it seemed, in a house with fiancé number one, fisherman/supermarket heir Kent Leppink. Leppink had bought the place with his own money.

Everyone knew everyone else in Wasilla. The place was all of five square miles in size. Neighbors talked about how when Leppink left on a fishing trip, men would come and go from the house he thought was his and his alone with Mechele. Both fiancé number two John Carlin III and fiancé number three Scott Hilke visited and stayed there at various times.

Hilke, of course, had already been eliminated as a suspect in the Leppink murder by the state police. Hilke was just another guy, one of many, who fell under Hughes's spell. But when Kent Leppink found out about the other guys, all hell had broken loose. Kent Leppink wound up murdered, his body dumped in rural Hope, right across Turnagain Arm.

Some eighty miles away by car, Hope had been a rural enough place to dump a bullet-riddled body with the hope, no pun intended, that no one would find it for quite some time. It was a logical assumption ruined by a random maintenance check by Chugach Company lineman Jim Hardy. When he found Leppink's body sprawled beneath a power line within forty-eight hours of death, his discovery spoiled that part of the murder plot.

The state police had formed a theory—Mechele Hughes and fiancé number two, John Carlin III, had lured fiancé number one, Kent Leppink, out to Hope. There, he was ambushed and shot in the back. When he whirled on impact, Carlin, who was probably the shooter, put one in his chest. The last shot in the cheek, with powder burns no less, was meant to finish him off if he wasn't already dead.

Considering the killer had been wielding a .44 Magnum of still unknown origin, it might be considered a bit of overkill. Maybe even personal. Further investigation had also shown that while she had originally said she was out of town when the homicide occurred, Hughes had arrived back in town with more than enough time to take an active part in it. Yet again, Hughes had been out on the local firing range practicing with a "big gun."

After the body was found in Hope, the trail had led back to Wasilla, where the Alaska State Police had confronted Mechele Hughes and John Carlin III. They were in the midst of searching Leppink's belongings at the loving couple's Wasilla home. Now *that* was interesting. They hadn't been officially notified by anybody that Leppink was dead and they were already combing over his belongings for . . . what? Perhaps evidence of their guilt? Or maybe the guy just stuffed money in his mattress.

What was becoming clear was that if Hughes and John Carlin III had conspired to kill Kent Leppink, the conspiracy began in Wasilla. Until 1992, Wasilla had no police department of its own. It relied almost completely on the state troopers for all its law enforcement functions. But on October

3, 1992, by a slim margin, Wasilla's voters approved a new sales tax to finance the town's first-ever police department.

" 'I'd feel safer saying this if the margin was wider, but I think Wasilla finally sees the light. People see the need for change,' said Sarah Palin, 28. Palin, a political newcomer, who was one of two supporters of the police–sales tax plan elected to the city council Tuesday," the *Anchorage Daily News* reported.

Four years later in the summer and fall of 1996, as the Alaska State Troopers continued the Kent Leppink homicide investigation, the Wasilla Police Department had grown to include uniformed cops, one investigator Jean Achee (pronounced "Ah-shea"), and at the top, chief of police Irl Stambaugh. With suspect Mechele Hughes already fleeing across state lines, the last thing the cops needed was politics interfering any further with "clearing" the Leppink homicide.

It happens.

In August 1996 Councilwoman Sarah Palin announced her candidacy for mayor of Wasilla. While Alaska tradition is for city elections to be nonpartisan, the state Republican Party ran ads that highlighted her conservative stance on major issues. Palin's campaign circulated anti-abortion fliers throughout the town. Simultaneously, she highlighted her church work as a born-again Christian and her National Rifle Association membership. Perhaps she ran into Kent Leppink at some of those meetings; he was an NRA member too.

On October 2, Palin beat incumbent mayor John Stein. The final tally was 617–413 in Palin's favor. Out of a total of 1,030 votes cast in the small town, Palin won by a "landslide" of 200 votes. Moving swiftly, on October 26 Mayor Palin sent resignation requests to all the city's top managers to resign their posts. Her stated purpose for the unusual action was to test their loyalty to her new administration.

One of her targets was chief of police Irl Stambaugh. A

former captain of police with the Anchorage Police Department, hired by Palin's predecessor, John Stein, he was perceived as Stein's "man" and, apparently, had to go. Next, Palin had a little talk with town librarian Mary Ellen Emmons.

According to former city officials and Wasilla residents, Palin discussed with Emmons the possibility of banning books Palin found objectionable, though it is not clear which ones Palin had in mind. Hopefully, *Lobster Boy* was one of them. Anyway, the librarian had the temerity to object. With this political firestorm surrounding it, the Leppink murder investigation continued with the cops just trying to do their job.

"The primary investigation for the Leppink homicide was by the [Alaska] Criminal Investigation Bureau," Jean Achee of the Wasilla Police Department recalled.

Achee's recollection is correct. While jurisdiction for the Leppink murder stayed in the hands of the Alaska State Troopers, the matter of local cooperation in investigating the homicide, *any homicide,* was of paramount importance.

"I was the only investigator for the town," Achee continued. "Back then, Wasilla was five squares miles."

It really wasn't much ground for a local cop to cover. In New York City, for example, five square miles would encompass more than a million people. In a populated section of Alaska like Wasilla, it was all of forty-two hundred.

"I knew Sarah Palin since she was a councilwoman. And as mayor she dealt with the police department all the time. She was the one who knew and kept our budget," added Achee, who now serves Wasilla as a police sergeant.

Asked if Mayor Sarah Palin would have known about the Leppink homicide, former Wasilla chief of police Irl Stambaugh replied:

"I would think so. Everyone watches the same stuff on TV and reads the same stuff. You couldn't have missed it."

The murder of a Wasilla resident like Kent Leppink was an almost unheard-of occurrence. A "body dump" job was even rarer. Usually in homicide investigations, the mayor of a small town would commit even limited resources to capturing and prosecuting the murderer of one of her own.

One way that is popular is to put up a reward for the arrest and prosecution of the guilty parties. Many times, the financial incentive alone, regardless of amount, causes those who know of the crime, and are perhaps protecting those close to them who have committed it, to turn and help the state. Juneau, Alaska, had found success with doing exactly that, a "Crime Line" number that people could call in to with tips on crimes and be eligible for a cash award.

A second method of assistance is even more basic.

Knowing that the state police have jurisdiction in homicides—and sometimes don't announce their presence when in town investigating—the mayor might simply ask the police chief and his force to cooperate with the state police in solving the homicide. Locals are usually best at interviewing neighbors who might be reticent to talk to "outsiders," state cops.

In an academic paper, "Effect of Local Police Presence on the Prosecution of Violence Against Women" presented at the American Society of Criminology annual meeting at Atlanta, Georgia, on September 4, 2008, the authors argued forcefully for the use of local investigators in major crimes in Alaska.

"Given the relatively small populations in rural Alaska, villages lack the economies of scale necessary for having fully trained and state-certified police officers posted locally on a permanent basis. Nonetheless, these [local] officers provide valuable assistance to troopers. Local police, with their understanding of local cultures, are better able to obtain cooperation for interviews and investigations, particularly to assist troopers in locating suspects, victims, and witnesses," the paper's abstract states.

But according to former chief of police Stambaugh, "I don't recall the Wasilla police ever being involved in the Kent Leppink homicide. I never had a conversation with Mayor Palin about the murder."

It was also possible that since this was the murder of a fisherman being cuckolded by the stripper, it was something best kept far away from anyone seeking a political career.

"I don't recall ever discussing the Leppink case with her [Mayor Palin]," confirmed Sergeant Achee.

At the time, Stambaugh was still having major problems of his own. On January 31, 1997, Mayor Palin fired police chief Irl Stambaugh and library director Mary Ellen Emmons. Immediately, Wasilla's citizens spoke out against Palin for firing Emmons due to the librarian's failure to agree to censor books. Palin backed down, putting the librarian's firing letter back in her holster.

Stambaugh wasn't so lucky. His firing stood while the Leppink murder investigation was stagnating. Making matters worse, even if the Wasilla police had tried to go to the media for help in solving the homicide, they couldn't. Palin had come out with a surprise executive order that was crystal clear: no city employee was to talk to the news media without her imprimatur.

Not bound by Palin's edict, however, the state police went public in an attempt to solve the homicide. On February 5, 1997, this story suddenly appeared in print in the *Anchorage Daily News*:

TROOPERS SEEK GUN IN SLAYING CASE
February 5, 1997

Alaska State Troopers are asking for the public's help to find the handgun used to kill a Wasilla man on the Hope Highway. The body of Kent J. Leppink, 36, was found May 2, 1996 . . .

If the state police could find the .44 Magnum that killed Leppink—the murder weapon—they had a good shot at tying it into the murder directly by a few means, including ballistics, fingerprints, and DNA. The problem was getting anyone to pay attention to their plea for help buried on an inside page amid the front-page coverage Mayor Palin had created with the Stambaugh firing and Emmons firing/re-hiring.

Stambaugh then sued Palin, accusing her of "contract violation, wrongful termination and gender discrimination." The city had to use its money to defend that lawsuit, which it eventually won. By March 1997, Wasilla was receiving applications for the open position of chief of police. It's hard to steer a ship without a rudder, or a police department without a chief. Mayor Palin's political machinations with her former chief of police had the effect of making it difficult for the rudderless Wasilla Police Department to fully assist the state police in tracking and gathering evidence that might have led to the resolution of the Leppink case before the millennium.

Carlin had also flown the coop, back to his home state of New Jersey. The state police found themselves whipsawed. The movies and television had done law enforcement a disservice. They made people really believe that cops in real life could force confessions out of suspects and have them stick. Well, maybe a few cops still did that. But detectives and prosecutors alike know that judges frown on such behavior and are just as likely to throw out a forced confession as to let it stick. Trial judges especially hate having a case overturned on appeal. A case in which a forced confession is allowed at trial is a prime target.

Forget the movies and TV. Only the stupid criminal gives police a confession. The smart ones, like Mechele Hughes and John Carlin III, clam up and get out of town. That's what they had done. Ever try extraditing a person from another state? Unless you have evidence that is overwhelming—read *direct*—there's little or no chance of getting that person back, political considerations, of course, notwithstanding.

Direct evidence, like fingerprints, DNA, eyewitness statements, or a confession tie the suspect in *directly* to the crime. Circumstantial evidence implicates without tying the suspect in directly. No one, for example, could say for certain without confessions that Hughes and Carlin planned and carried out Kent Leppink's murder. But the *circumstances* seemed to show they did. Still, a good defense lawyer would point out that without *direct* evidence, there wouldn't be much of a court case.

Or was there direct evidence, and it just hadn't been found yet?

How, then, to get a grand jury to indict with only circumstantial evidence? How indeed! The myth of the prosecutor being able to lead the grand jury by the nose and get it to do anything he wants is really that—a myth. While a grand jury will indict more often than not, especially in a conservative state like Alaska, that's with direct evidence or strong circumstantial evidence.

The Louisiana state cops were still on the trail. While passing through New Orleans to visit her mother, Hughes had had a little visit from troopers Schwartz and Frey. Executing a search warrant on her trailer, they had found and confiscated Kent Leppink's laptop computer. On it were e-mails that the cops said had been erased. The computer was sent back to Anchorage. It was uncertain who had erased the e-mails, though Mechele Hughes was suspected. The cops also suspected there was something *directly* implicating her in those erased e-mails.

There they went again—suspected. Not good enough for an indictment. It would have been nice to have the technology to go into the hard drive and find the erased files. Unfortunately, the state troopers didn't have it. To think that every state had the forensic expertise in 1996 and 1997 to find erased files on a hard drive is naïve, just as even today many states do not have the technology to track serial killers.

No, to break the Leppink case, the state needed direct evidence like the murder weapon. Tie Hughes and/or Carlin into possession of the murder weapon, and that would lead to a murder indictment, maybe even a conviction.

In an effort to find out what former Wasilla mayor and present Alaska governor Sarah Palin knew or did not know about the Leppink murder investigation in 1996 and 1997, she was contacted through the following Web site: http://gov.state.ak.us/govoffices. The Web site states categorically:

> Alaska law prohibits use of state equipment or resources for campaign or partisan political purposes. Please do not send any messages to these addresses or make calls to these telephone numbers concerning campaign or partisan political activities. Information about elections and candidates can be found by calling, writing, or e-mailing a campaign office for that particular candidate.

Since the questions to be put to the governor had to do with her service as mayor and nothing do with her nomination by the Republican Party in 2008 to be vice president of the United States, she was called at her Alaska office.

"We have no information about her before she was governor," said press officer Aron Burkett. "I think you have to call the campaign number to get more information."

Asked what that number was, Burkett replied:

"We had a number but it's been disconnected. We don't have any further information," and she hung up the phone.

Given the opportunity, the questions to ask Mayor Palin are as follows:

Are you aware of the brutal homicide of one of your fellow Wasilla residents, Kent Leppink, in 1996?

Did you ask Chief Irl Stambaugh to assist the state police in their homicide investigation?

Did you offer a reward for the arrest and prosecution of Kent Leppink's murderers?

There is no record that shows that the Wasilla Police Department spent one dime, one penny, investigating the Leppink homicide and assisting the state police.

"The state police ran out of resources and the case went cold," Stambaugh recalls, as cold as Leppink's body in the ground. But even cold cases come out of the ground to haunt the guilty. Sometimes it just takes time.

For Mechele Hughes, it was time to build a whole new life.

CHAPTER

6

This is investigator Preston Wade. I'm interviewing Brian Brundin, B-R-U-N-D-I-N. His date of birth is October 11, 1939. Now you called in connection with the demise of Kent."

"Leppink, yes," Brundin answered.

Preston Wade didn't know he was about to run out of resources. That's generally not something cops know in advance. Wade was on the murder until his superiors at the Alaska State Police pulled him to work another case, or the overtime pay ran out, whichever came first. Or the case just ran cold.

He certainly was aware of what was happening on the political scene in Wasilla; how could anyone not be? Chief Stambaugh had wisely pointed out that everyone read and saw the same thing in the Anchorage area. The *Anchorage Daily News* was the local paper. The networks all had affiliates operating out of Anchorage, plus the usual plethora of radio talk shows.

Palin's politics was news; the Leppink murder investigation was not. It was that simple. Except for the lone story in the *Anchorage Daily News* in February, it received no media coverage whatsoever. That helped in some ways. It's always nice when the prime suspects don't think you're after them but you are.

Sure, Hughes and Carlin had gone out of state. But that didn't mean the murder investigation didn't continue. You still needed evidence to prosecute and there was still precious little, at that.

"And I understand he was a client of yours?" Wade continued.

"That's correct," said lawyer Brundin.

"When did you first meet him?"

Brundin hesitated.

"I can tell you anything because ah . . ."

"Okay," said Wade gently.

"My duty to Kent is now gone. He's dead. Anything he's told me is not privileged."

Brundin was reminding himself of that as much as the cop.

"I brought my file with me to help," he finally said, pointing to it. "He first came in saying he wanted a fishing boat set up, with he and his fiancée Mechele."

He consulted it for a minute.

"Mechele Kay Hughes, that's M-E-C-H-E-L-E Kay Hughes. It was February of '95. He came in to have me set up for him a corporation. To own a fishing boat he was going to buy. Then at a later time, she was to have nothing to do with the fishing boat, and primarily because his father was doing the funding for him."

"You set it up then?"

Brundin nodded.

"I did that."

"So, Kent wanted to set up a corporation for his fishing

business. And he wanted to include Mechele. But when his father became the financier of the operation why did he not want to include her?"

"I think Kent thought throughout that his father put the money in that he should have to be on the corporate board. He had first rights and so forth, to make sure the investment was protected."

Made sense. Leppink had embezzled money, so his father would want a tight leash. But it also sounded like Leppink was trying to show some heretofore unseen responsibility to both his family and himself. He had really grown during his time as an Alaska fisherman. He had taken his final opportunity in the Last Frontier to do what so many others had before him—he had reinvented himself. But like any person, he still had flaws.

"Was there any hardships that you're aware of because she was, tentatively, going to be part of the corporation and then she was removed later?"

Wade was fishing for motive. Maybe even hoping.

"It seemed strange to me," Brundin answered after a while. "I just had an impression that his father and mother didn't necessarily like Mechele."

"When you started the corporation and he came, did you meet his father and mother?"

"Never have."

"Then how did you get the impression that they didn't like Mechele?"

"Just from what he said. He seemed to be torn between the notion of including his fiancée first in his corporation and then in his will. Later on he made her the primary beneficiary of his will. And then he came in and tore his will up. And this is a very recent occasion and that's where I think I have a better feeling for their relationship."

"When was it that he had you make out a will?"

Brundin rifled through the papers until he found what he needed.

"He asked me to do it last fall. His instructions to me last September were he needed a will."

September, six months before the murder.

"His dad was to have control over the company until the note was paid off," the lawyer continued. "Then he wanted his fiancée Mechele Kay Hughes to be the sole beneficiary."

Good ole Kent! He had found a way, if he survived, to reward Mechele. And if he didn't, he had his insurance policy—the letter to his father.

"But his father was to be the personal representative until he is married. He put his real estate in Mechele's name. He wanted to continue his durable power of attorney to his father. He had no children."

"Then what happened?"

"He came in on the fifteenth [of April]. My notes show he was in from ten forty-five to twelve-fifteen."

Ninety minutes.

"He came in with Mechele. First time I saw her. She had a bandage on her nose. Operation of some kind."

Probably a nose job, the cop thought. She got Leppink or someone else to finance it.

"Then he signed his will. I think he brought her in because he wanted to show her that he was gonna make the primary beneficiary. Apparently, he told her that."

"And you discussed the will with her?"

"Yeah, she sat there on the sofa and he just sorta dropped in with her. I printed up a copy of the will on the computer, made a couple of small changes on it, and they had a conversation going which was kinda strange."

"Strange?"

"She was angry that his father had suggested a prenuptial

agreement. She couldn't understand why in the world his father would do that."

Maybe to protect his son?

"It upset her. But Kent was a very mild man. He didn't really carry on an argument with her." Then things got a little bitter. "I could tell something was going between them. There had apparently been some affairs going on and she made a comment that really struck me."

"What was that?"

"She said, 'I don't know if I can compete if it wasn't a girl.' That suggested that she caught him in some homosexual relationship. Anyway, he signed the will."

Once that was done, Mechele Hughes was the $1 million beneficiary on Kent Leppink's life.

"The next day, he showed up again in the morning and he was quite upset. He wanted to know if he could sue Northstar Hospital. He'd gone there to inquire about the fact that Mechele had been to Northstar and to get some counseling himself."

Northstar was known for its counseling programs.

"So he came in with this notion that Northstar had violated a confidence. It was in that conversation that my notes say as follows: 'Mechele had an affair then a second affair with a guy they're living with.'"

That would be Carlin. That's how she came to go to Northstar. "Her boyfriend's son was getting counseling there. She talked like the boy was her stepson. She used his last name for things, Carlin C-A-R-L-I-N. Since I had just seen him the day before, I asked him what was going on with this fiancée of his. I've seen a lot of marriages come and go, and it didn't look like he was headed to a happy one."

That's when Brundin told Leppink the story of the scorpion riding on the back of a turtle across a river. Even though the scorpion promises not to sting the turtle, he does it anyway, midway in the water. When asked why he would do that, given that the turtle would die and therefore the scorpion too, the scorpion replied:

"I can't change my spots, that's who I am, I'm a scorpion. I am what I am. And in that conversation he told me that Mechele was living in town with Carlin who has a son little John. While Kent was fishing last summer she had an affair with him [Carlin]. Then they had a home in Wasilla. It was being renovated. John was doing some of the work. So they were both living in John's house here in Anchorage. And he thought the affair was still going on. She denied it."

"Did Kent say anything else?"

He said that John was giving her money. That she had a habit of "spending her credit cards right up to the limit, he was giving her money and gifts. I suggested to him that men don't give women gifts for nothing. "

That's when Brundin said, "I caught that comment yesterday, where she said something to the effect that you were having an affair, maybe with a man."

"What did he say?"

"He did not respond to me, so I have no idea what his reaction to that was. He didn't wanna talk about it and I didn't force the issue with him. I just told him to calm down that he didn't have a lawsuit against Northstar. He should really think about his relationship because it looked to me as a third person who saw it that his relationship with Mechele was going absolutely nowhere and he ought really give that a lot of thought."

"Then the next time he shows up again was the twenty-sixth of April?"

"He came in again unannounced; there he was! He was upset again. He said that he woke up this morning, she borrowed his car last night, also took his computer, a ten-thousand-dollar computer, plus stuff from his storage shed, which included a bronze statue worth four thousand or more, two antique rugs. 'Can I call the police?' So we had a conversation about he knew where she was; he didn't. And he had already gone to his insurance agent that morning and changed his beneficiary."

"She was apparently the sole beneficiary on an insurance policy."

"On his life."

"So he had changed that prior to coming to your office that morning?"

"That's what he said, or he was headed to do it. He asked how he could do that and I said the way to end it is to tear it up and he tore it up in front of me and I threw it in my trash can. Which meant the prior will was back in being. His prior will was done where he comes from and names his family as beneficiaries."

"How was Mechele acting when you were first making out the will with her as the beneficiary?"

"My impression now is that she, ah, desires things."

Wade snickered.

"And wanted things from him."

"Was John giving her gifts?"

"Yeah. Paying off her credit cards and that sort of thing."

"Did he ever say how John was getting his money?"

"Nope, never did. They were just living in John's house while their place in Wasilla was being fixed."

"Did Kent indicate where he was getting his money?"

"I think it was from fishing." Again, that made sense. "Anyway when he came in on the twenty-sixth and tore up his will, he said his dad would arrive that day. He was gonna talk to him about all this. As of this morning, I've talked to a lawyer for his dad. He says his dad and mother received a letter from him that was marked open if something happens to me. It is a grisly letter, detailing his relationship with her."

Preston Wade was not about to comment on that, at least not on record. He knew, of course, that what Brundin was saying was true. But he could not acknowledge that because the letter was evidence in a murder investigation. Instead, something else occurred to him.

"Did Mechele have an attorney with her at any point in time that you're aware of?"

"Yeah, the notion was that I might represent the both initially. I never have represented her. And when they signed the will, she suggested she might like one with a will and tryst. I gave her a confidential questionnaire for information, but I've never had a relationship, ah, as lawyer to her."

From the surface, it would appear Brundin was lucky he didn't have any relationship with her. The men in Mechele Hughes's life seemed to wind up having a bit of trouble.

Brundin added, "I don't know that she's represented by anyone else. She never mentioned it."

"Did Kent ever talk to you about the insurance policy, about how much it was?"

Wade was going for the gold, the motive in Leppink's death.

"I think so," Brundin answered slowly, thinking back on it. "Let me look." He rifled through his papers. "You're welcome to copy my file." Brundin coughed and continued to look.

"I have another question."

Brundin looked up.

"You said earlier that there was, that Kent placed all his real estate in her name and stuff. If there's other real estate, I don't have a list."

Brundin didn't know of any other coowned real estate, "Except the house in Wasilla I understand they have."

Wade asked him how much the policy was for. Brundin rifled through his papers.

"I don't have it written down," he replied

"Hey Brian," Wade asked, taking another tack, "you said that Kent had come in when he changed his will and he was upset about Mechele taking his computer and his car, apparently, and this bronze statue. Did he happen to say how he knew that it was Mechele that had done that?"

"No. He said he woke up that morning and she was gone."

"At any time, particularly on April 26, did Kent in that conversation ever express to you any concerns he had about Mechele or John Carlin possibly wanting to harm him in some way?"

"No."

If Leppink had expressed his "concerns" about his safety to Brundin, put that together with the letter and they had a nice ribbon and bow underneath a nice murder one indictment.

"When he left your office, was there any indication from Kent what he was gonna do next that day, outside of possibly canceling or changing the beneficiary on the insurance policy if he had not already done it?"

"Yeah, I think he already did it. He was gonna go pick up his dad at the airport. What he wanted to know was if he could go to the police, and I said, 'Do you know that she in fact took something?' He really didn't know."

That was unfortunate. If he had made a felony complaint, the police would have had to investigate. The fact is cops don't need "evidence" to investigate; that's the way lawyers think. The truth is cops need evidence for an indictment.

"Was that the last time you saw Kent?"

"I saw him for only fifteen minutes."

And he never saw him alive again.

"Now is there anything else at all you can think to add, Brian, or do you think we've covered what you wanted to make sure we knew?"

"I think I've covered everything that might bear on the potential of someone wanting to hurt him."

"One more question, Brian, if you don't mind. Did she ever make any telephone calls in your office inquiring at any time after the will was made whether the will had been changed at all?"

"Nope."

Now how would Columbo handle that?

"Ah, it slipped my mind. Do you know whether Mechele was aware he destroyed the will [naming her as a beneficiary] on the twenty-sixth?"

"He was angry with her, he may well have told her."

Then Brundin backed off from that statement.

"He didn't say he was gonna tell her he was looking for her, he wanted to find her."

"Because she had taken off the night of the twenty-fifth?"

"Yes, he woke up that morning and she was gone."

"So I take it, Brian, that contact you had with Mechele on the eighteenth—"

"The only time I've seen her."

"And you've had no phone conversations?"

"No conversations, no nothing."

"Anything else."

Brundin was silent.

"All right, the time is now approximately eleven thirty-seven. I think that'll be the conclusion of the interview."

After it was over and Brundin had left, Preston Wade reflected on their interview.

The motive for Hughes wanting Leppink dead was clear—the $1 million life insurance policy on which she was, or so she thought, the sole beneficiary. Wade supposed that Carlin was indeed the proverbial triggerman, but there was no direct evidence to tie Carlin in yet, except that he appeared to be controlled by Hughes in some way. Was that the deal? This Hughes broad was so good in the sack that men just lay down and died for her? You had to wonder what it was that drew men to her like the proverbial moth to the flame.

Evidence, *dammit*, he needed direct evidence to back up Leppink's written statements. From the grave, Leppink, God bless him, had done something totally unique—he told the cops who his murderers were. He had laid down that gauntlet to whatever police officer, bureaucrat, or anybody else in power in Alaska came across his note.

Now that was a piece of direct evidence. No doubt. It identified the dynamic duo to the state of Alaska and told the state to do something about that. Now that is a nice piece of direct evidence. But you needed something to back it up. If a prosecutor could prove it in a court of law, he had two murder one convictions. But to do that, he would need that goddamn direct evidence . . . Hughes's expensive tastes!

If he could show a pattern of the stripper using Leppink, aka fiancé number one, and then making fiancé number two want to kill for her, that would be a case of the facts perhaps leading to two first-degree murder indictments.

Since this was Alaska, where there are no counties—none are needed in such a barren land where populated areas are few and far between—there would be no fight for jurisdiction. It lay with the Alaska State Police and always would. But they needed a stronger case to indict. The word of the decedent, no matter how rational he might appear to be, was not enough.

It was going to take a lot more investigation to even get to an indictment.

CHAPTER

7

By 1996, the Internet certainly existed and some computers had access to it. Then vice president Al Gore, a future Nobel Prize winner, claimed publicly that the Internet was a brainchild of his. It was especially popular among academics, who had been among the first to take advantage of the medium's research resources. Search engines were of course more primitive than they would eventually become. This was still before the Internet took off. But regardless of the time in which the crime is committed, nothing could ever compensate for shoe leather. It's the cop's best friend.

Nothing quite matched shoe leather for getting information. Sandy Pryor's was the third jewelry store in Anchorage that Preston Wade strolled into. The interior was typical, with cases of rings, crosses, pendants, earrings; rubies, diamonds, opals, and emeralds safely ensconced inside locked glass cases.

"Hi, my name is Preston Wade; I'm an investigator with the state police."

He flashed his badge.

"What I was wondering was if either of these two people ever came into your store?"

He showed her pictures of Leppink and Hughes. She remembered him immediately.

"Yes, he came into the store," Pryor confirmed. "He was very nice."

"Did he buy anything or just look around?" Wade asked.

"He came in and wanted to buy a pair of opal earrings and a pendant. He was very nice. But—"

"But what?"

"She came in later to exchange it."

"Who's she?"

"The woman in the photograph you just showed me."

Wade showed her the photograph of Mechele Hughes again to make sure the identification was correct.

"That's her, like I said," Pryor quickly replied. "One of the reasons I remember is because she came in afterwards."

Hughes wasn't happy with Leppink's purchase.

"She returned the items because she said the earrings were uncomfortable. I gave her a credit for it because she didn't choose anything else that day."

"Did she ever come in again?"

"No, but Mr. Leppink did."

"For what?"

"Another purchase."

"Which was—"

". . . either a diamond ring or a diamond pendant. I don't recall which one."

"Did Mr. Leppink say anything when he bought it?"

"He made a statement that he planned to give it to his fiancée, Mechele Hughes."

"Was that it?" Wade asked.

"What do you mean?" replied Pryor, confused.

"Did either of them come in again?"

"No, but their friend did."

"Their friend?" said Wade, trying to hide the surprise in his voice. "What was his name?"

"John Carlin. [He] said he purchased the ring for Mechele Hughes. He [Carlin] came in and asked to look at a D flawless diamond." Undecided, he left, but "He came in the following day and asked to purchase it."

The stone itself, a loose diamond, would cost $11,000. The stone was set in a platinum solitaire ring as an engagement ring. Its appraised value, Pryor said, was $17,000.

"Did he say who he purchased the ring for?" Wade asked.

"Mechele Hughes," Pryor answered.

So that would make Carlin fiancé number two to Leppink's fiancé number one, with Scott Hilke bring up the rear as fiancé number three, though Hilke had not bought her a ring.

"Can I borrow your Yellow Pages for a second?"

Pryor pulled it out from under the counter and handed it over. Wade figured that if Hughes went for one kind of luxury she probably went for another. He checked through a phone directory and found a couple of furriers nearby.

"Thanks very much," said Wade, handing her the directory back.

Back on the street, Wade checked two of the furriers in the area and came up with nothing. He struck gold at the third shop, Schilling and Rosen Furriers. Like most furriers, there was a nice showroom at first when you walked in. Behind that in the back was the shop. In the shop, the "nailer" nailed the animal skins with staples onto a board, following the designer's pattern. Then the nailer would wet them down, so the skins would stretch.

When they were dry, the nailer would take the skins off the board, being careful to remove all the staples. Once that was done, the garment was given to the "operator." This was a sewing machine operator who expertly sewed the skins together to make them into a coat, a stole, a hat, or whatever it was the customer wanted.

Seal coats had been popular at one time but with the ban against hunting them, most furriers relied for pelts on mink, chinchilla, and if you wanted to go cheaper, beaver, rabbit, and, since this was Alaska, moose. Despite the shop being in the back, Wade could still smell the wet fur. It was a not entirely unpleasant odor, but he couldn't imagine what hard work it was nailing down those skins.

The saleswoman in the showroom was Betsy Johnson. Once again, Wade introduced himself, flashed the tin, and showed the pictures of Leppink and Hughes. Johnson gazed at them for a few moments.

"Yes, I remember this man coming in, Mr.—"

"Leppink."

"Leppink. Yes, he came in to purchase some items."

"Do you remember what they were?"

"Furs."

Furs? Looking for something a little more specific.

"Could you take a look at your receipts," Wade asked, "and tell me what exactly it was that he bought?"

Johnson checked her records. Leppink had bought a fur.

"How much did he spend?"

"One thousand dollars."

That wasn't chump change.

"May I look at the record of purchase?"

"Sure," and she handed over the receipt.

According to the receipt, Leppink had written a check for Schilling and Rosen Furriers in the amount of $1,000 all right. The money came from a joint account Leppink had with Hughes. Both their names were on the check.

"Did he come in to purchase anything else?"

"No," said Johnson, shaking her head.

"And this woman," said Wade, holding up Hughes's picture, "did she come in with him or alone at any time?"

"No, she didn't. I never saw her."

"Is there anything else you can remember about him or the purchase? Anything he might have said?"

"Just that Mr. Leppink said he intended to give what he purchased to his fiancée, Mechele Hughes. He was very specific about that."

"Did he ever come in to buy anything else?"

Johnson shook her head.

"Well, thank you very much for your time," said the cop.

As Wade left, he was wondering how much stuff Leppink had actually bought for Hughes. He seemed to be a very conflicted man, on one hand trying to please her, to buy her love perhaps, but on the other, distrustful that the love was truly real. How many guys had been in the same situation, or was that a sexist thing to think?

Not in this case. Carlin was playing along with Hughes on what appeared to be a totally different network. He too was a fiancé. It generally wasn't a good idea to get two guys together who wanted the same girl and were trying to in some way pay for her. That was a guarantee for violence.

Back at the office, Wade called Shelby, Michigan, and got Kent Leppink's mother, Betsy Leppink, on the line. Wade asked her about the expensive purchase her son had made for his fiancée.

"I remember that my son showed me a diamond pendant one evening before we were to dine with Mechele at Elevation 92," Betsy Leppink said.

Located in Anchorage on West Third Avenue, Elevation 92 was a really nice restaurant. Each table has a view of the Knik Arm inlet, though most of the tables also faced the port's industrial area. The bar served a full plate of hors d'oeuvres that a diner could make into a meal. It included such varied delights as oysters, sashimi, and crab-stuffed mushrooms. Washed down with a wide variety of wines, it would make a wonderful dining experience if you didn't have more important things on your mind like the engagement of your son to a stripper.

Betsy Leppink couldn't recall any other luxuries that Mechele Hughes might have worn. So Wade turned to Hughes's asset, the house in Wasilla where they had lived "together," the house that was undergoing some sort of repairs to make it more habitable. It all sounded sort of fishy.

Looking at the note that Leppink had sent his parents, Wade focused on a line that said, "Gary Brooks would like to own the Togiak. Give it to him if you can, otherwise, sell it to him so that he can afford it. Owning the boat might make a difference in his life."

What a curious thing to say. At the end of his life, Kent Leppink was thinking about redemption, perhaps for the money he had embezzled, perhaps for some other unknown reason. It certainly sounded like Brooks was a friend, but nevertheless he might have some information.

"Mr. Brooks, my name is Preston Wade," he said over the phone, "and I work for the Alaska State Police. I'm an investigator looking into Kent Leppink's murder."

After talking for a few minutes about Kent and what had happened to him, Wade turned the conversation toward the stripper.

"The house in Wasilla that they shared. I understand Kent put a lot of money into it."

"Yes he did," Brooks confirmed. "Kent said that he spent between $47,000 and $53,000 remodeling the place. It was Hughes's home but Kent didn't hesitate to give her the money."

Free and clear. No note, no loan, no nothing. Hughes didn't owe him a dime, but she did owe him respect, which she clearly did not have. No, Wade realized, he wasn't being sexist. Leppink was a "sugar daddy" to Hughes in the best or worst sense of the term. He gave her money and gifts in return for companionship and sex. Wade had to wonder if this was a pattern—had she done this to other men?

John Carlin was clearly one of them. Up front, he'd probably ponied up more cash and jewels for his maiden. Leppink's insurance money made the difference. What made it interesting was that Carlin and Hughes knew each other well before Leppink took out his insurance policy, and that both could have wanted him dead for their own reasons. If that was true, they had executed a successful murder conspiracy. Premeditated murder is also referred to as murder one, a crime in Alaska punishable by death. If the stripper was ever charged and convicted of that crime, she'd be doing one hell of a dance into the death chamber.

Hughes, of course, would claim that all of this, the investigation, Leppink's note to his parents, was all a farce, a carefully executed plan by Leppink to hide one essential fact about his life from everyone. Hughes had claimed in police interviews that Leppink was gay, that all the talk of marriage was simply a ruse designed by Leppink to keep his sexual preference from his parents. But if that was the case, why spend so much money? On a ruse, especially when the guy didn't have that much, just to fool his parents, whom he seemed to be especially close to?

Suppose instead that the opposite was true: Kent Leppink was straight. To himself, he wasn't being a "sugar daddy" at all. He really loved Mechele. But the common sense his father had instilled in him had told him that to Mechele, it really wasn't love at all. That's why he suspected that Carlin had ulterior motives. Kent Leppink was as conflicted as any man can get when he's in love with a woman, especially one he suspected was going to kill him.

Killing for money is biblical, one of the oldest motives for murder. In fact it made no difference whether Kent Leppink was straight, gay, bisexual, or into bestiality. This was Alaska, where the Old West notion of justice still applied: in the end it was all nonsense. The only thing that counted was solving the murder and bringing the gal, the guy, or whoever had done it in to face a court of law.

Courts of law, of course, needed evidence. Direct evidence. What about the gun? *Where the hell was the Desert Eagle?* Pursuant to a search warrant, the cops had searched Carlin's home, but it was nowhere to be found. They had found in his house a gun case that would fit a Desert Eagle but it wasn't specially designed for it. It could fit any gun or guns of similar size.

The cops also searched Mechele Hughes's car. Discovering a gun holster, they seized it as possible evidence, but again, there was nothing specific to tie it to the Desert Eagle. Neither case nor holster contained the firearm. So where was it, down a sewer someplace, at the bottom of Turnagain Arm, or maybe someplace in the woods in Hope?

Wade recalled that Decristofario, the manager of the Anchorage shooting range, had claimed that Hughes had used a .44 Magnum for target practice. Hughes never denied using the weapon at the range, claiming she wanted proficiency with the firearm so she could get a concealed weapons permit. That begged the question of why a stripper wanted a gun and whose gun it was. A good defense lawyer, Wade knew, could easily argue she needed a gun for protection from overeager customers, not to mention the fact she left the club every night with a lot of money for her work. Anyone with a load of bills on him is a target for a mugger.

Going through the notes on the case, Wade found that another officer, Stuart Bailey, had gone back and interviewed Scott Hilke about Carlin's gun.

"I saw the gun," Hilke told Bailey. "It was huge, black, and a semiautomatic." That matched the description of the Desert Eagle perfectly. Looking through his notes again—really glamorous police work—he read about Bailey's conversation with the employees at Johnson RV Center in downtown Anchorage.

"Gene Collins, a salesman at Johnson RV was contacted by John Carlin III in connection with purchase of a motor home," Bailey had written in his notes. Carlin then returned with Hughes and John IV. According to Collins, it was clear that John Carlin III was buying the motor home for Mechele. "Mr. Collins followed John Carlin and Mechele to Wasilla where they wrote up the papers."

Carlin III "paid approximately $18,000" down on the brand-new RV. "Hughes financed the remainder of the RV's cost for $57,000. Delivery occurred on June 7, 1996." Oh, she had the money from stripping, lots of it. But it was highly doubtful, now, that Johnson RV would get the rest of their payments with Hughes on the run.

Stu Bailey had also checked on the exact route of the RV. Since she was driving south, she had to go through Canadian customs, who had been notified of their road trip. Besides Carlin's seventeen-year-old son, Hughes was carrying some exotic birds that she favored. Unsurprisingly, they were stopped by the Canadians at the border.

Stu Bailey was called by Inspector Philip Girard of Canadian customs. He reported that the motor home was searched when crossing the border. Without a warrant for her arrest, Hughes and her menagerie were allowed to pass into the Lower 48 at Blaine, Washington. Apparently strange birds, even when coupled with the prime suspect in a murder, were not enough to stop her from reentering the United States.

On June 27, Wade was contacted by Bobbi Randolph; she lived down the block from Carlin III in Anchorage. She said that there was a large moving van and a green Jeep outside the Carlin residence. Based on information she had provided, Preston Wade contacted World Wide Movers, Inc., in Anchorage and talked to Jake Gibson. Gibson told him that the company was loading up property right then from the Carlin residence at Brook Hill Court. The movers were using a tractor and a trailer to load all the stuff in and get the job done.

"Where's the stuff bound for?" Wade asked over the phone.

"I think the ultimate destination of the household goods is New Orleans. Mr. Carlin inquired about the cost of shipping to New Orleans."

That figured; Hughes's hometown. Her mother was there and so were friends and family.

"After the tractor and trailer are loaded, they will be at World Wide Movers, Inc., at Hart Street in Anchorage pending further arrangements."

For the cops, "further arrangements" would be a search warrant into a black hole.

According to NASA, "Black holes are the evolutionary endpoints of stars at least 10 to 15 times as massive as the Sun. If a star that massive or larger undergoes a supernova explosion, it may leave behind a fairly massive burned out stellar remnant. With no outward forces to oppose gravitational forces, the remnant will collapse in on itself. The star eventually collapses to the point of zero volume and infinite density because no light escapes after the star reaches this infinite density, it is called a black hole."

But contrary to popular myth, NASA is quick to point out,

"a black hole is not a cosmic vacuum cleaner." It was the same thing in homicide. "Cold cases" don't get sucked into a black hole. They go cold because leads peter out and the prosecutor doesn't have a good case to prosecute.

Murder suspects do try to go through the holes in the net that the police extend out for them, or can extend out for them. Then there are the constitutional holes. Those are the ones that the critics of the Leppink case would rail against in 2008. Rail, all they want, it was as simple as the following:

AMENDMENT V

No person shall be held to answer for a capital, or otherwise infamous crime, unless on a presentment or indictment of a grand jury . . .

AMENDMENT VI

In all criminal prosecutions, the accused shall enjoy the right to a speedy and public trial, by an impartial jury of the state and district wherein the crime shall have been committed, which district shall have been previously ascertained by law, and to be informed of the nature and cause of the accusation; to be confronted with the witnesses against him; to have compulsory process for obtaining witnesses in his favor, and to have the assistance of counsel for his defense.

No matter who or what Mechele Hughes was, no matter how innocent or guilty the police thought she was, they were bound by those two amendments to the United States Constitution. Once a suspect has flown, driven, rowed, or ridden thousands of miles south to the Lower 48 or any other place for that matter, it's impossible to get him back without a strong warrant for murder. And if he happens to fly the coop to a country that has abolished capital punishment and means it, including most of the countries in the northern hemisphere, extradition can get pretty dicey.

That is if you're a state like Alaska with the death penalty. But that was a long, long, long way off. The first thing the Alaskan authorities needed was to convince a judge to give them a warrant to extradite a person who now resides in another state back to Alaska for murder. So what really did the Alaska State Police have to show the judge?

It was a strong circumstantial case. There was motive (the insurance money) and means (Carlin and his gun). A computer check through secure government databases showed that Carlin was a former Marine marksman. Oh yeah, there was also opportunity—the note authored by Hughes and Carlin that lured Leppink out to the middle of no place where he got three slugs in his body.

So what really happened? Why did the state of Alaska suddenly abandon the Kent Leppink murder investigation sometime in 1997? No one's talking. The state troopers won't comment on it. Neither will the prosecutor. Repeated attempts to communicate with them have been cordial, but they have never answered specific questions.

Clearly, the case against Mechele Hughes and John Carlin III was purely circumstantial. The direct evidence provided by the missing gun would help. Even someone who had seen either or both suspects with the gun would help. But nothing had shown up . . . yet. Cops always have hope.

Even with the state's limited technological resources, the computer check in 1996 allegedly yielded certain incriminating e-mails that had not been erased. These were not documented, however, until 2008. But whatever they had, it wasn't enough for indictments. This was 1997. There were still eleven years of history to go.

Preston Wade began to realize that neither Mechele Hughes nor John Carlin was going to be indicted for Kent Leppink's murder, not anytime soon. Like a true police professional, he moved on to other cases that needed him, and had been stacking up on his desk.

But Kent Leppink never wavered far from his mind. Wade promised himself that if he ever again got an opportunity to get the guy justice, he would go out of his way to do it.

PART II
Louisiana Gumbo

CHAPTER

8

Gumbo is as much a part of Louisiana's history as Thomas Jefferson's Louisiana Purchase. This traditional dish of southern Louisiana goes further back historically than even the bargain Jefferson struck with the French in 1803. The culinary delight of gumbo is a dark soup, thick with rice, vegetables, seafood or meat. It's characterized by this kind of variety of ingredients though two things remain constant in all gumbos—rice and a thickener, usually some sort of roux that the chef concocts. That's what makes it all come together.

Like a good Louisiana gumbo, Mechele Hughes could at times be a variety of things—loving, nasty, generous, mean, and affectionate. But something was missing in the gumbo that would turn her into what she wanted to be—a metaphoric roux that would turn her into a rich woman with nothing to worry about. During 1997 when Mechele Hughes was visiting New Orleans, she finally was able to put together the metaphoric roux that would bring her gumbo of a life together under the identity of "Mechele Linehan."

Some who knew her would later characterize it as a complete personality shift. It wasn't. She actually began acquiring the essential ingredients of her roux when she left home as a teen under her sister's identity.

New Jersey

Jersey Joe, an expert on NJ lifestyles and geography, grew up in Weehawken. Across the street was Hoboken.

"The home of Frank Sinatra, the sign used to say and still does," says Joe. "That sign was one of my fondest memories, that and going down to the strip clubs in Bricktown. That's what the locals called it, Bricktown," Joe continues.

Brick Township is a township in Ocean County, New Jersey, directly north of Atlantic City. Being on the beaches of the Atlantic seaboard, most of the area north of the East's gambling capital is devoted to summer tourism. People like to walk the area's old-time boardwalks; eat cholesterol-clogging food, chewy taffy, cotton candy, and every kind of custard imaginable. There were other things that were really tasty but you had to go past the rides to get to them.

Moving south on the boardwalk, the rides, oh the rides! There's one, the pirate ship, that uses a cam to go so far up, a really tough true crime author got an anxiety attack! The others are a bit tamer, with their electric lights flashing through the darkness, the boardwalk lit up like Christmas in July, and the beaches warm during the day and cool at night; the waters, well, that was a different story.

Sometimes medical waste, tar, and unknown substances washed up on the beaches and the waters would suddenly be pronounced "polluted" by local politicians, and the beaches would be condemned as unsafe for swimming for a few days. Life would sometimes imitate art, again, when rare shark attacks in the areas waters would cause the beaches to be shut down for a few days, just as in *Jaws*. Just as in *Jaws*, regardless of the problem, the beaches would be reopened quickly. It was summer, for God's sake! Tourism is what helped the people survive, so the beaches remained open.

Brick Township didn't have any of those problems. While Brick Township is located on the mainland, Beaches I, II, and III are situated on the Barnegat Peninsula, a long, narrow barrier peninsula that separates Barnegat Bay from the Atlantic Ocean. After hovering for years in the top five, in 2006 the 76,119-person township earned the title of "America's Safest City," out of 371 cities included nationwide in the thirteenth annual Morgan Quitno survey.

Back in the 1980s and early 1990s, guys like Jersey Joe went down to the seedy strip clubs in Brick. That's where they would see Mechele Hughes slithering down a pole, gazing at them with eyes that made their cocks jump almost as fast as their wallets. The clubs were all the same—the area in front where the poles were and the girls stripped, the chairs surrounding the stage; the chairs and tables farther back around the perimeter of the club; and in the back the "private area," where the girls would do lap dances on guys with the provision the guys couldn't touch certain areas—tits and pussy.

Mechele Hughes, though, had a life away from the strip clubs. For four years she lived with Pat Giganti. A native New Yorker raised in Manhattan, currently in the building business, Giganti had gone across the river and settled in Brick. He fell in love with Mechele Hughes, who was twenty years his junior.

"Oh yeah, she took money off me," Giganti said like it was yesterday. "But it was like she had a split personality. She could be so sweet and then turn around and screw you."

In those days, Giganti was a young man in his thirties from Manhattan, seeking his fortune across the Hudson

River in New Jersey. He fell in love with a teenage Mechele Hughes, who by then was consciously aware of what riches her face, body, and most importantly her very force of being could help her accumulate.

Mechele Hughes and Pat Giganti lived together for four turbulent years. After they split up and Hughes moved to Alaska, they had no contact. A decade later, out of the blue, she would call him with a request, for the sake of old times.

Washington State

The state of Alaska's later contention that the Kent Leppink murder plot was based on *The Last Seduction* was not entirely accurate.

"Bridget Gregory has a lot going for her: she's beautiful, she's intelligent, she's married to a doctor."

That's the first line of IMDb.com's synopsis of journeyman director John Dahl's critically acclaimed *The Last Seduction* (1994). Starring a smoldering Linda Fiorentino, the film borrowed the plot of Billy Wilder's classic 1944 masterpiece *Double Indemnity*, about a married woman who charms a man into a murderer who kills her husband, an oilman, for his insurance money.

In their version, Dahl and screenwriter Steve Barancik made the husband a doctor. The insurance policy and the man who is duped into murder remain the same. If the prosecutor's theory of the crime was correct, then it would become no accident that Mechele Linehan was beautiful, intelligent, and yes, she did marry a doctor, just like Bridget Gregory.

Two versions emerged of how Mechele Hughes met her future husband, Dr. Colin Linehan, United States Army. The first is the briefer. While in New Orleans, Hughes went back to stripping at a Bourbon Street Club. She gyrated her way into a new life with a combination of pelvic thrust and pole slithering, her million-dollar smile, curvy body, and sheer presence.

The second version is the one Mechele Hughes claims publicly and what she has acknowledged about her movements after she left Alaska in 1996. She was a bright young woman—no one doubted that—saving all that money from stripping to go back to school! Here's how one of her lawyers described it in a brief:

"After her departure from the state, Hughes returned to school for which she had been saving money. While attending Loyola University in New Orleans, she met Colin Linehan. Still, Ms. Hughes continued her volunteer work even while attending school by volunteering at the Audubon Zoo."

Volunteer work? In between showing her bush at the Bush, Hughes had allegedly worked as a volunteer in various Alaska charities. Apparently, none of the men in her Alaskan life knew she was a closet humanitarian and intellectual, anxious to gain academic honors.

"The couple [Linehan and Hughes] was married on May 31, 1998."

Hughes took her husband's name, and Mechele Hughes literally disappeared into thin air. That was it right there. Who she was, her suspected criminal activities in Alaska, all seemed to disappear into the ether behind her. By using a different name, she conjured a different personality, directly at odds with the stripper cum killer. She became the doctor's wife, a role she performed well.

It was a similar situation to that of Sara Jane Olson. Formerly known as Kathleen Soliah, the Symbionese Liberation Army domestic terrorist hid out for twenty-four years as a Minneapolis soccer mom without her husband knowing about her past, until the day the law finally came calling in 1999. It seemed that on April 21, 1975, the SLA robbed the Crocker National Bank in Carmichael, California, killing forty-two-year-old Myrna Opsahl. A mother of four, she was in the process of depositing money for her church.

Getaway driver Patricia "Patty" Hearst first told police that Soliah was involved in the robbery and murder. Hearst then claimed Soliah kicked a pregnant teller in the abdomen, leading to a miscarriage. Soliah pleaded guilty to murder and attempting to bomb Los Angeles police cars in 2001. Released by accident a year early on March 21, 2008, the next day she was about to board a plane for Minneapolis when the cops realized their mistake. They stopped her and put her back in for the last year of her sentence.

By separating out the two parts of her life into two different identities, Linehan might have succeeded even longer than Olson had by staying invisible. Sure, it was easy for the cops to find her, professionals, but what good would it do without *direct evidence*?

"After the couple moved to Maryland in 1998, Mechele Linehan continued pursuing her Bachelor of Arts and Bachelor of Science degrees at Howard County Community College and at the University of Maryland."

No one pursues a bachelor's degree at a community college. Community colleges award an associate's, or two-year degree. The credits are then transferred to a four-year school as Hughes probably did. As for the claim she was pursuing a B.A. and B.S. simultaneously, that sounds more like the indecision of a typical college student.

"In the next three years she continued her volunteer work as a CPR instructor for the Red Cross, and as an after-school science teacher assistant with the Howard County School District." Still a prime suspect in a murder case Mechele Linehan, aka Hughes, became an instructor to children in a publicly supported school system.

"Linehan also worked to support her schooling both as a nanny for two different families, and as a waitress at two different restaurants. In June, 1999, Audrey Linehan was born."

Mechele Hughes became a mother! A year later the family moved to Olympia, Washington, where Dr. Linehan worked as a civilian doctor at Madigan Army Medical Center in Tacoma.

"During the next few years, Linehan raised the couple's daughter and continued to pursue her schooling and her volunteer work. In 2001, she received her Bachelor of Arts degree from Saint Martin University. In 2004, she received her Masters in Public Administration from Evergreen State College."

A Benedictine-run university, Saint Martin's was in Lacey, close to Olympia where Mechele Linehan lived. The place was small, about nineteen hundred students total, emphasizing liberal arts. The college became Saint Martin's University in August 2005, "to more accurately reflect the institution's nature, better fulfill its mission and recognize the wide variety of undergraduate and graduate programs available to students," according to its Website.

Evergreen State College in beautiful downtown Olympia was the place Linehan chose to pursue her graduate studies. The college's "Master of Public Administration Program provides high-quality professional education to students pursuing careers in government agencies, nonprofits, tribal governments, and research and advocacy organizations. Effective advocates for change."

Its Web site also states, "Evergreen's MPA program is unique, due to our emphasis on social change and democratic governance, and the College's innovative approach to education. The cornerstones of an Evergreen education, graduate or undergraduate, include collaborative and interdisciplinary teaching and learning, narrative evaluations instead of grades, and an emphasis on experiential learning and engaged discussions encompassing diverse views."

While pursuing this degree, "She also found time to volunteer at the Olympia Crisis Center, at Saint Michael Parish and at her child's school when Audrey began attending school." Linehan seemed bound for some career, perhaps in nonprofits. "Mechele also continued to work for the Washington State Executive Ethics Board and during this period . . . purchase an existing business and launched a new facility/business with A&L Enterprises, LLC, a laser and skin clinic/treatment centers."

Mechele Hughes as Mechele Linehan had seemingly redeemed the life she had left behind. She was still a prime suspect in a murder case, but she had never been charged with a crime and she had no reason to believe she would be. In her years in Olympia, she had gained the confidence, respect, and love of her neighbors, who saw her as devoted wife and mother. She became the June Cleaver of Olympia, Washington. That's the way it looked to neighbors and friends.

The problem was, perfect mother June Cleaver was never the prime suspect in a murder. Regardless of the name she now went under, Alaska had not forgotten Mechele Hughes. Far from it. The case that the Alaska State Police referred to as "the black widow" remained high on the list for reinvestigation. That, however, required funds.

Enter Bill Bratton, the patron saint of modern policing, and especially cold case squads.

There was no choice for an enlightened democracy than to form cold case squads.

Primarily, cold case squads are formed in a jurisdiction that is plagued by a significant number of unsolved murders. Some cold case squads are formed because the volume of new cases or police initiatives prevent any work from being done on old cases. Then again, some squads are formed when murder rates decline and departments have adequate resources to start investigating old cases.

Across America through the turn of the millennium, the rate of homicides and other crimes declined significantly. To a large extent this was due to Bill Bratton and the innovations he brought to police work that were copied all over the United States.

Bratton established an international reputation for reengineering police departments and fighting crime in the 1990s. Bratton first led the Boston Police Department, where he cut crime sharply. Moving south like Red Sox free agent third baseman Wade Boggs, who signed with the Yankees, Bratton signed first with the NYC subway police and then moved over to head the NYPD as police commissioner. In those two posts, Bratton revitalized morale and achieved the largest crime declines in New York City's history. How he did it was with CompStat.

Bratton led in the development of CompStat, the internationally acclaimed computerized crime-mapping system developed by the NYPD in the 1990s and now used by police departments nationwide, including Alaska. By bringing all crime and arrest data together by category and neighborhood, CompStat revolutionized policing. Armed with real-time information, accurate intelligence, rapid deployment of resources, individual accountability, and relentless follow-up, CompStat enabled officers to focus their efforts in problem areas.

By the beginning of the millennium, Bratton's CompStat so dramatically reduced the rate of homicides, it opened up funding nationwide, including Alaska, for cold case squads. Every cold case squad operates under the same guiding principle of American jurisprudence.

Since the nation was fortunate enough to have such a righteous man as George Washington, our first and some historians believe our greatest president, murder has been the only crime that has no statute of limitations. Therefore, the police, county—as it happens Alaska has none, but that's another story—city, state, and Federal, are at any time free to go after a suspected murderer. All that is necessary is the will and the way, or, put another way, the bucks from taxpayers to finance the operation.

Cold case squads are actually good investments for taxpayers because they get big bang for the bucks. They are paying not for simple law enforcement, which any goon can do, but intelligence—the ability to take evidence, including decades-old body fluid, bones, flesh, witness statements, and, using new technology developed over the past decade, get that evidence to speak in a different way, get the evidence to find the bad guy, bring him in, get him tried and convicted.

Every cold case squad reviews and continues the investigation of unsolved homicides or suspected homicides. "They can be especially useful in locating and working with past and potential witnesses and reviewing physical evidence to identify suspects. The squads may investigate unsolved homicides currently assigned to a homicide detective when deemed necessary by supervisors—usually when the lead detective has exhausted all leads," according to the Bureau of Justice Assistance.

The most important component of cold case squads is personnel; the squads must have the right mix of investigative and supervisory talent. The staffing model used for cold case squads is determined mainly by whether the squad works full- or part-time and whether it is based within a police agency or a prosecutor's office. Cold case squads can consist of any of the following:

Single full-time investigator.

Squad of two or more full-time investigators.

Investigators working on cold cases in addition to other investigative duties.

Former homicide detectives in a part-time or volunteer capacity.

One-time cold case squads assigned to high-profile unsolved cases.

Occasional squads.

Investigators in a special squad based in a district attorney's or state attorney general's office.

County/regional cold case squads.

As needed, the squad could use the services of the Federal Bureau of Investigation (FBI) and U.S. Marshals Service, though this is generally frowned upon for the primary reason that the Feds are rarely accepted by local cops. They just don't like them let alone trust them. When they are, outreach is more likely to the U.S. Marshals Service, an agency that, while it receives its fair share of criticism, still had the grudging respect of local law enforcement.

Under the Judiciary Act of 1789 which President Washington championed, the office of U.S. Marshals Service was established to "support the federal courts within their judicial districts and to carry out all lawful orders issued by judges, Congress or the President." The service received its greatest renown in post–Civil War America when the marshals brought to ground the greatest outlaws of the Old West. By the twenty-first century, the marshals morphed into a group of trusted officers who, among other things, protected judges threatened by right-wing political groups and ran the Witness Protection Program for Federal witnesses whose lives were in danger.

In contrast, the FBI was not formed until an act of Congress in 1935. Under the leadership of J. Edgar Hoover, it immediately gained a reputation for flashy, high-profile cases by going after the outlaws of the 1930s. The agency eventually became known for its sense of superiority over local law enforcement, more style than substance. The agency's well-documented subsequent failure to act on intelligence it had in advance of the 9/11 plot led to its reputation being in tatters. As they got going, cold case squads developed their reputation with substance over style.

"High priority was generally given to cases in which witnesses could, in the present, identify suspects; information or evidence can identify possible suspects; or the initial investigation identified witnesses who could not be located or needed to be reinterviewed. Cases of moderate priority include those in which preserved evidence can be processed and analyzed through modern technology (such as an automated fingerprint identification system, DNA analysis, or DRUGFIRE, a computerized program that tracks signatures on spent shell casings), and whose status as a homicide can be reclassified depending on the results of the additional laboratory analysis," the Bureau of Justice Assistance continued.

Cold case investigators begin by reviewing the actual case file, talking with all previous investigators tied to the case who might be alive, and getting any documentation not in the case file. Investigators are particularly looking to review or locate any gaps of information in the case, including people mentioned in statements that do not have a corresponding interview report in the case file, undocumented investigative actions (such as search warrants without documentation of service), and so forth. Any available evidence is assessed for future usability and additional analysis. The original suspect is rarely reinterviewed.

After reinterviewing significant witnesses and working all viable leads, if no suspect can be identified, the detective writes a summary documenting the follow-up investigation and recommending either further investigation or inactivation. A homicide case can be closed either through arrest of the suspect or by administrative action. The arrest of a suspect renders a case closed regardless of whether the suspect is convicted or even brought to trial. A case may be closed administratively if the suspect for which the department has probable cause either has died or has been prosecuted for another crime and is behind bars for life.

Cold case squads reviewed and prioritized according to the likelihood of an eventual solution. Cases that generally received the lowest priority were those in which no known physical evidence or witnesses are available to help identify a suspect. The highest priority were those cases in which the murder victim, like Kent Leppink, had been identified; the death was ruled a homicide; suspects were previously named or identified through forensic or other methods; an arrest warrant was either issued or seriously considered; significant physical evidence such as fingerprints, DNA, or shell casings can be reprocessed for further clues; newly documented leads have arisen within the last six months; and critical witnesses are accessible and willing to cooperate.

The genesis of Alaska's cold case squad began in July 2003, when Captain Matt Leveque was assigned as commander of I Detachment, with a mission to facilitate the reorganization of the Criminal Investigation Bureau into the Alaska Bureau of Investigation. Most states had already formed cold case squads, and Alaska had finally caught up to the curve. The idea now was to become a cohesive state-wide bureau offering closer support to trooper detachments and local police departments like Wasilla's.

As part of this new mission, a cold case squad was formed, with three investigators assigned for the entire state. One was stationed in Anchorage, a retired Anchorage Police Department (APD) sergeant, Linda Branchflower. The two stationed in nearby Soldotna included Preston Wade. He had retired as a sergeant of the Alaska State Police, but had read-ily come out of retirement at the chance to crack some old cases, especially one that had never left his mind.

It all sounded good in theory, didn't it? A second crack at the one that got away. Preston Wade was a long way from getting a conviction. But when he was finally able to turn to "the black widow case," he was determined that this time around, he was going to get the direct evidence to convict Hughes and Carlin. The Alaska State Police knew where Carlin was too. He had remarried and was living in southern New Jersey, the kind of place Jersey Joe says it's pretty easy to get lost in.

The Alaska cold case squad was really a group of men and women who most resembled *Double Indemnity*'s Barton Keyes, the insurance investigator who had a "little man" in his stomach that told him when there was a murder being perpetrated. Collectively, the cold case squad had a stomachache because of what they referred to as "the black widow case."

The black widow was Mechele Hughes. The only thing that would make their stomachs feel better was an arrest and, more importantly, a conviction.

CHAPTER

9

2004

Preston Wade didn't have to go back to his notes or any of the reports from the eight-year-old homicide. Kent Leppink was no colder now in his grave than he had been a decade ago when three rounds from a .44 Magnum had "dropped" him. That was what Carlin had said he wanted the gun for; to "drop" a bear. Instead, it had been allegedly used to "drop" a human being, thirty-six-year-old Kent Leppink was in the prime of his life.

It was post–9/11 and the United States was in the second year of the Iraq War. John Kerry was running for president against the incumbent George W. Bush, and most people seemed to be focused on that. The Alaskan investigators had their own feelings about those events and kept them to themselves. Their job was to solve the case. As for those who had been directly involved with Kent Leppink, the time between the murder and the present had been hell.

They didn't have to go to Iraq to see it; living with an un-solved murder in your family is exactly that. Someplace in their minds, Kent Leppink was still there. His parents Ken-neth and Betsy, his brothers Craig and Ransom still grieved for him and wanted his murder solved.

Conscience. Where was the conscience? Preston Wade took a second look at the case and thought it might reside with John Carlin IV. He would now be a twenty-something. Carlin IV had not originally been interviewed because his father had prevented it. Maybe he knew something he wasn't supposed to tell. Wade made a note to have him in-terviewed.

The motive had been clearly established and would be at any of the trials: the $1 million life insurance policy. Yes, Leppink had changed the beneficiary, but there was no evidence to show that Hughes knew that, and by extension Carlin. Therefore the motive was money. Okay, fine, there's motive. What about opportunity?

Wade figured they had it covered with the phony note that Carlin wrote to lure Leppink out to Hope and his death. The state still could not explain the actual transportation situa-tion, that is, how did Leppink's car get back to Anchorage if he was dead, unless someone drove it? That would imply two people on the scene, the other to drive the car that had brought them there. Then again, maybe Hughes dropped off Carlin in town, Carlin flagged Leppink down when he saw him—not difficult to do in a one-horse town—and then Carlin drove out with Leppink to mile marker 13.5 and gunned him down.

Direct evidence, the gun, it all came back to the missing murder weapon. That was the one piece of evidence needed to connect Carlin, and by extension Hughes, to the homi-cide. Wade looked over his notes from eight years before.

The gun could not be found. A thorough search of the

Hope crime scene by the Alaska State Police criminalists brought the shell casings that identified the missing murder weapon. A search of the premises of the Anchorage home where Hughes and Carlin were living had included a gun case as part of the confiscated evidence. What went in the case? A gun. That was obvious. Big deal. What good was the case without the specific gun? It had to be the specific one. Even if they found that John Carlin had an antique a Colt .44, it made no difference. That wasn't the murder weapon.

Wade took a step back.

Supposing the murder weapon was effectively disposed of. Anchorage, Hope, Wasilla, all the same, surrounded by water, mountains, woods, endless places to get rid of a gun. It was a miracle they had found the body at all. If the gun hadn't been found by now, it wasn't going to be. What Wade did know was that the Desert Eagle was a very rare gun because of its limited production, making limited availability. That had been established early on.

Alaska is farther from the continental United States than Hawaii is. That's why prices are so high. About everything had to be shipped in; almost everything is made other places. Including guns.

That was it! That's what he had missed back in '96. The murder weapon, the .44 Magnum Desert Eagle, had come into Alaska, probably from the Lower 48 or Hawaii. Therefore, one of two possibilities:

John Carlin III brought it with him to Alaska when he immigrated in 1994.

John Carlin III bought it in Alaska.

A quick check of the records showed no record of Carlin bringing a pistol with him to Alaska. He also had no pistol permit on record. That of course was not to be expected if it was a weapon that was going to be used in a homicide. A weapon bought specifically to commit a homicide. The assumption was that the weapon, bought before the homicide, was used by Hughes at the local firing range. They had the firing range instructor's interview verifying that.

"Linda," said Preston Wade to Alaska State Trooper Linda Branchflower. "I'd like you to research the classified ads in the *Anchorage Daily News*. What you're looking for is someone selling a Desert Eagle .44 Magnum prior to the Leppink murder."

The *Anchorage Daily News* has one of the best online archives of any small paper in the United States. Branchflower accessed the classifieds in the newspaper. It was careful, patient research, looking through old ads of people selling everything from cradles to guns. Oh yes, guns. Lots of ads for guns. Shotguns, pistols, revolvers, automatics, and then there it was.

There was an advertisement from 1995. Someone was selling a Desert Eagle. Branchflower called the number; it was an old cell phone number, no longer active. But cops can do stuff regular people can't when investigating a homicide. The cell phone company was contacted and the identity of the person who bought that number was ascertained. The man's name was David Stilchen.

Branchflower tracked Stilchen down. He was a serviceman who went back and forth from Alaska to the Lower 48. Stilchen told the investigator that in 1995 he sold his .44 Desert Eagle, a case with holster, belt, and ammo pouch to a person "Meeting the description of John Carlin III." They also had the gun case, which Stilchen later identified. That was very, very good.

The identification of the gun case, and what it held, the

alleged murder weapon, bolstered Stilchen's identification of Carlin III being the guy who bought it from him. It was always hard to know how something would play before a jury. They were presented with both the prosecution and defense's version of events. Wade knew that with what they now had, they could get an indictment.

Still not good enough. There was one other piece of evidence that had never been examined: Kent Leppink's laptop computer. The technology now existed to access anything that had been erased on the hard drive. Wade got Leppink's computer out of evidence storage and lined up his forensic computer expert. With the proliferation of computers across the United States from the mid-1990s and into the millennium, the position had now become a police staple.

The Alaska Department of Public Safety maintains its own laboratory where forensic analysis of computers takes place. It's a peculiar specialty that requires the skills of a police investigator and a computer expert at unlocking secrets, sometimes from long ago. Investigator Christopher Thompson was that expert.

"On 3–22–04, I was assigned to conduct a computer examination as part of a homicide investigation. Information provided on the case by Investigator Branchflower indicated that the computer to be examined, a Gateway Solo Laptop, had been seized from Mechele Hughes who had been involved in a relationship with the victim in the case. The computer had belonged to the victim in the case. Hughes was also considered a suspect," Thompson subsequently wrote in his report.

A search warrant authorized the examination of the computer and the zip disks for electronic evidence related to the homicide. When Thompson opened the case, "inside were a total of eight 3.5 floppy disks. These disks were later protected, then examined and found to be various program disks. The case also contained a power cord, a smaller case containing a printer cable and connector, an owner's manual; a modem, a 3.5 inch floppy disk drive and a single page of paper with instructions. The zip disks were each encoded in a plastic case."

Leppink was nothing if not neat. Even Hughes's attempts to access the computer and its drives had not obliterated the evidence he had left behind. Mr. Leppink had been a very clever guy. Opening up the computer, Thompson accessed its components. "The computer was found to contain a single hard disk drive. This hard drive was removed from the computer and was connected to a forensic computer using a device called Fastbloc manufactured by Guidance Software. This device prevents data from being written to the hard disk drive being examined thus preventing the alteration of data contained on the disk."

In other words, nothing taken off the computer would be altered by the police. The defense would never be able to claim they had done something to taint the evidence. Aren't computers wonderful?

"A duplicate image of the hard drive was then obtained by using EnCase Forensic Edition Version 4.17b software. The hard drive was then disconnected from the forensic computer and reinstalled in the laptop."

Thus the chain of evidence was maintained. Now, Thompson really went to work.

"I numbered the Zip disks in sequence p1–8, placing a corresponding adhesive label on each of the disks. A digital photograph was taken of the disks." Again, chain of evidence. "The data contained on the Zip disks was imaged following the procedure outlined by Guidance Software."

That meant he finally got to see what was on the disks. The process involved using EnCase for DOS version 7.10 software to acquire the data on each of the disks. Prior to the acquisition, the software allows the investigator to "lock" the disk so that it is not written to, and therefore data on the disk is not altered.

Perfect! Chain of evidence maintained right down the line. So what the hell was on it? Thompson's report is almost taunting in its exactitude.

"The image obtained of the hard disk drive was examined using EnCase Forensic Edition software. The disk contained Windows operating system software and various program and data files. Within the file structure was evidence that America on Line (AOL) was being utilized as an email program," said Thompson.

Lips licking . . .

"There were a number of deleted email messes which were recovered to various degrees by EnCase software."

All right already!

"These emails appear to be to and from the various parties associated with this case to include Kent Leppink, Mechele Hughes, Scott Hilke and John Carlin. A number of the email messages which appeared to be between Hughes and Leppink made mention of a receipt for life insurance and Leppink's attempts to send a copy of the receipt to Hughes."

Sure enough, Leppink had scanned in his receipts. Thompson found "a scanned copy of two receipts for insurance with the New York Life Insurance Company. The receipts bore the names Mechele Hughes and Kent Leppink. This document is printed and attached to this report."

As he looked through the zip narratives in his office,

one caught Preston Wade's eye. "Akmewell" was Hughes's online ID, while "TangoPI" was Leppink's.

4/2/96

From "Akmewell" to "TangoPI"

HEY I GOT A MIN TO WRITE YOU. I JUST WANTED TO SAY YOU KNOW I LOVE YOU AND YOU KNOW OUR LIVES WILL BE FINE. WE HAVE MANY THINGS TO DO AND SAY TO ONE ANOTHER. I HAVE A LOT OF THINGS TO DO BEFORE WE SETTLE DOWN SO PLEASE STOP SNOOPING AND ASK-ING ALL OF THOSE QUESTIONS. I AM SERIOUSLY TELLING YOU THIS. . . . IF YOU CONTINUE TO RUMAGE THREW [SIC] MY PRIVACY AND SNOOP THREW MY BELONGINGS I WILL NOT MARRY YOU. WHILE WE ARE NOT MARRIED, NOTHING IS YOURS. DO YOU GET IT?

WHEN WE GET MARRIED YOU CAN KNOW WHERE EV-ERYTHING IS IN THE HOUSE. BUT THEN YOU GO THROUGH MY PURSE AND MY BAGS. YOU ARE INVADING MY PRIVA-CY AND I WILL NOT TOLERATE IT. SO REMEMBER I THINK YOU OWE ME AN APOLOGY. I DID NOT TAKE YOUR PHONE BOOKS AND I TIRED [SIC] TO LOCATE IT AT THE AIRPORT BUT IT WAS NOT TURNED IN.

I MAY COME TO FLORIDA AND SEE YOU AND YOUR FAM-ILY IF YOU ASK ME NICELY. STOP DEMANDING YOUR SHIT ON ME. I AM SICK OF IT. YOU TRY TO TELL ME WHAT DAY I HAVE TO MARRY YOU. GET OFF YOUR HIGH HORSE. YOU HAVE WAITED THIS LONG YOU JUST CAN CALL IT OFF IF ANOTHER TWO WEEKS REALLY CRAMPS YOUR LIFE. I WILL NOT GET MARRIED UNDER THOSE CIRCUMSTANCES. I AM FINALLY TELLING YOU THIS BECAUSE I LOVE YOU AND YOU NEED TO KNOW THAT YOU HAVE BEEIN PISSING ME OFF.

YOU HIDE SO MUCH SHIT FROM ME, HOW DARE YOU QUESTION ME? YOUR SAFETY DEPOSIT BOXES YOUR HIDDEN SHIT YOUR STORAGE SHED ETC., ETC., ETC. I NEVER PRY INTO YOUR SHIT EVEN WHEN YOU HAVE TAKEN MY SENTIMENTAL PRIVATE BELONGINGS AND BROUGHT THEM TO YOUR STORAGE.

THAT WAS STEALING AND IF YOU WANT TO MARRY ME THEN YOU NEED TO REALIZE I LET THAT GO. YOU STOLE FROM ME AND I DID YOU WRONG TOO. YOU CONTINUE TO SNOOP AND PRY. STOP, IF YOU WANT ME TO HAVE YOUR CHIDLREN AND SPEND THE LIFE TOGETHER THAT WE HAVE TALKED ABOUT THEN YOU NEED TO KNOW THESE THINGS YOU ARE VERY CLOSE TO DRIVING ME AWAY.

ONE THING I WANT YOU TO KNOW IS I DO NOT WANT YOU TO BUY A HOUSE AND I DON'T WANT YOUR PRENUPTUALS. I HAVE MY OWN HOUSE AND IF IT IS NOT GOOD ENOUGH FOR YOU THEN YOU BETTER SACRIFICE YOUR HIGH HONOR FOR THIS WEDDING. YOU HAVE MADE ME SO ANGRY BY DOING MANY THINGS THESE PAST FEW WEEKS THAT I AM FED UP WITH. YOU WERE SO NICE BEFORE I AGREED TO MARRY YOU.

Mechele Hughes was actually telling off the guy she and Carlin, the state would claim, intended to murder. What was actually happening was that prior to the May murder, as Wade saw it, Hughes was putting still more pressure on Leppink and he was taking it.

YOU HAVE NO RIGHT TO QUESTION ME ABOUT MY FAMILY. UNFORTUNATELY, THEY ARE NOT CONCERNED AND I DO NOT WANT THEM INVOLVED ANY MORE THAN WHAT I EMPLOY THEM INTO. SO YOU CAN STOP SENDING MY MOTHER CARDS. DO NOT SEND HER CARDS AND YOU WONT EITHER IF YOU ARE PART OF ME. I DO NOT INTERFERE

WITH YOUR FAMILY UNLESS I AM ASKED OR TOLD I MAY
UNTIL I FEEL THAT I AM EXCEPTED [SIC] AND PART OF THE
FAMILY I WILL NOT EMBARRASS MY SELF BY FORCING MY-
SELF ON YOUR FAMILY.

That sounded like an interesting family relationship.

YOU NEED TO REMEMBER WHERE YOU MET ME AND STOP
AND THINK IF I WANTED MY FAMILY IN MY LIFE. THEN WHY
WAS I IN ALASKA AND DANCING WITH NO FAMILY THERE.

Possibly to snare a guy in a life insurance scam? Wade
had to wonder. Yet while allegedly plotting murder, Hughes
was emerging as a class-conscious snob, though she clearly
was in no position to look down her nose at anyone.

I THINK IT IS VERY OBVIOUS I DON'T CARE HOW YOUR FAM-
ILY AND BROTHER HAVE TURNED OUT. THAT IS NOT THE
SAME REASONS AND MAYBE ONE DAY YOU WILL KNOW
AND UNDERSTAND. UNTIL THEN, PLEASE DON'T MEDDLE
IN MY FAMILY RELATIONS. YOU CANNOT REPAIR THEM.
    WHO I INVITE WILL HAVE TO BE EXCEPTED [SIC] BY
YOU AND YOUR FAMILY. IF NOT THEN I WILL BE HEART
BROKEN AT THE ALTERNATIVE.

Sounded like a threat to call off the marriage if she didn't
get things her way, putting more pressure on Leppink.

MAYBE YOU SHOULD EXPLAIN TO YOUR PARENTS. TELL
THEM I HAVE VERY FINE LINES THAT DETERMINE THE
BOUNDRIES [SIC] OF MY LIFE. AND WHEN SOMEONE VI-
OLATES THEM, I HAVE THE OPTION TO ELIMINATE THEM
FRM [SIC] MY LIFE. THAT IS MY CHOICE.

Mechele Hughes had written in an e-mail to Kent Leppink that she would "eliminate" anyone from her life that violated her boundaries. Perhaps an innocuous statement, but this time it took a decidedly deadly turn.

There was an e-mail seemingly in reply from Leppink, but it was to John Carlin III at jarcarlin127@aol.com

> FROM THE MOMENT I MET MECHELE AT THE BUSH, I FELL IN LOVE WITH HER. IT WOULD SEEM PRETTY STRANGE TO SAY THAT, KNOWING WHERE SHE USED TO WORK. BUT WHEN SHE WOULD DO TABLE DANCES FOR ME, I WAS WATCHING HER EYES/ SURE, IT'S HARD NOT TO SEE THE NAKED BODY IN FRONT OF YOU, BUT I FELT MORE OF HER THAN JUST AS A SEX OBJECT.
>
> I KNEW THAT WE WOULD BE MARRIED TO EACH OTHER ALMOST FROM THE BEGINNING. I GAVE HER A DIAMOND ONE MONTH AFTER WE HAD MET. WE TALKED ABOUT LIFE TOGETHER. SEX. WAITING FOR AWHILE, HAVING CHILDREN, ETC. I WOULD HAVE MARRIED HER RIGHT THEN AND THERE, BUT WE TALKED AND DECIDED NOT TO SET ANY DATE RIGHT AWAY.

Not until the policy was in place? Kent Leppink was a sap, a really big sap. While the murder plot was being hatched, he was expressing his undying love for Mechele to Carlin, the guy the state theorized shot him.

> IT WAS ABOUT THIS TIME THAT SCOTT CAME INTO THE PICTURE. I WAS TOLD [by Mechele] THAT SCOTT WAS JUST A FRIEND AND THAT HE WAS GAY: "YOU HAVE NOTHING TO WORRY ABOUT TT." AND I REALLY DIDN'T WORRY ABOUT IT. I'M SUPPOSED TO TRUST THE ONE I LOVE AND BELIEVE EVERYTHING SHE SAYS.

Kent Leppink had placed his trust in the wrong place. Wade figured that between the e-mails, the note to his parents, and most importantly the almost direct evidence of the gun, it was finally time to go to the DA for arrest warrants. It was still basically a circumstantial case but a good one that might yield a conviction or two.

Dear Mechele,

The roof on your cabin in Hope is finished. It will not leak anymore. The fireplace has been cleaned but as he said, it will have to be redone within the next year or two. It is safe for you to use now. I also had all the locks changed and the key is under the stone by the tree, where the old key was. It has dead bolts now as well, so you will feel safe when you are there. The one key is universal and will fit all the door locks. I could not find someone willing to go to Hope and clean it though, so it will still be a little dusty. Also, the window screens are all fixed so there will be no mosquitos that will get in. I believe they are coming out now and are very hungry for fair skin people such as us. I am glad that I bought it for you now. It does make a fine getaway. I think when you come back from there this weekend, I would like to spend a couple of days there myself, if that is okay. I need time to figure out where I am going with my life when I sell the house. I have been thinking of Australia, if the Costa Rica deal doesn't look inviting and I don't like it. I sure am going to miss you but I know if something happens or you become unhappy here, you will call me and we can spend time together where ever I am at. You know how much I would like that. I do wish you all the happiness and joy in the world. I am sure you will be happy and raise a fine family. I do hate going and loosing you in my life thought. Please be well, safe and Happy. You guys enjoy your stay in the cabin this weekend.

With all the love I can have for a wonderful woman as you,

John

[handwritten note overlaid:] Great, please don't let anyone know where we'll be but you already know that. When Kelly the Elevator be roberts. And the back door does it close out there now? I don't mind you going out there now I don't mind you going out there now I do pled 4 it Sally I will clean it up nice. Don't worry about prying it cleaned. Love, and thanks again Mechele

The Hope note that lured Kent Leppink to his death

The body of Kent Leppink

The .44 Magnum Desert Eagle, of the type used to kill Leppink
(courtesy Magnum Research)

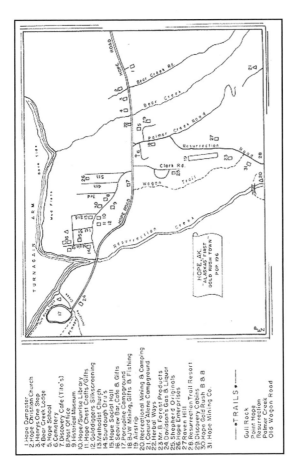

Map of Hope, Alaska, where Leppink's bullet-ridden body
was found outside the town
(courtesy Hope Chamber of Commerce)

Linehan and Leppink during happier days
(Bill Roth/*Anchorage Daily News*/MCT/Landov)

Linehan's lawyer, Wayne Fricke,
who headed up her defense team
(courtesy Wayne Fricke)

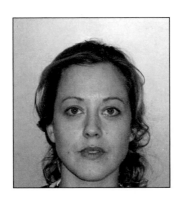

Linehan's Alaska booking shot
(courtesy Alaska Department of Corrections)

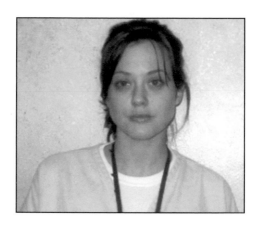

The stripper's booking shot after conviction
(courtesy Alaska Department of Corrections)

Scott Hilke testifying at Linehan's trial
(Erik Hill/*Anchorage Daily News*/MCT/Landov)

Mug shot of John Carlin III
(courtesy Alaska Department of Corrections)

Mechele Linehan listens
at her sentencing,
her husband Dr. Colin Linehan
sagging into her
as the verdict is read
(Jim Lavrakas/*Anchorage Daily News*/
MCT/Landov)

John Carlin III in prison before he was found bludgeoned to death on October 27, 2008

(Bill Roth/*Anchorage Daily News*/MCT/Landov)

B ack in rural Elmer, New Jersey, John Carlin III was shocked that the Alaska State Police had put out a warrant for his arrest. After learning of his arrest warrant on October 3, 2006, John Carlin III voluntarily flew back from Elmer, New Jersey, and turned himself in at Anchorage's courthouse on October 4, 2006. Mechele Hughes would have it a little different. The *Anchorage Daily News* bannered the headline two days later:

FORMER STRIPPER WANTED FOR MURDER IS NOW HOUSEWIFE, MOTHER

Just like the cops ten years before in New Orleans, police in Olympia, Washington, were forced to serve an out-of-state warrant on Mechele Hughes, now calling herself Mechele Linehan. The cops who came to her house found only her husband, Dr. Colin Linehan, at home.

Two years earlier, amid the crowd and cries of an estimated five hundred thousand protestors at the Republican

National Convention in 2004 in New York City's Madison Square Garden, Dr. Linehan's mother, Judy Linehan, was among those shouting, "No more Bush." In an article published in the *News Tribune* of Tacoma on August 30, 2004, she was described as follows: "Her son is opposed to the war, she said, explaining that she came to New York to protest 'because he has no voice.' "

Linehan had served his country as a military doctor in the Stryker brigade in Iraq. After leaving active service, he became a civilian doctor specializing in family medicine, at the Madigan Army Medical Center in Washington. With the cops at his door, he was shocked to find out what an Alaska State Police press release dryly described this way:

"On 9/28/06 an Anchorage Grand Jury returned secret indictments for First Degree Murder against John T. Carlin, 49, of New Jersey, and Mechele K. Hughes, 32, of Washington State."

The arrest warrants carried with them bail set at $500,000 each.

"You have one hour to find your wife and bring her to the station," said Deputy Sheriff Johnny McKay to Dr. Linehan when Mechele was charged. "We could do this in a small way, or in a big way."

Less than sixty minutes later, Mechele Linehan; her husband, Dr. Colin Linehan; and her lawyer showed up at the police station. Almost immediately, the case went national and the media ate it up. Reporters were dispatched to Olympia to do man-on-the-street interviews with people who knew Linehan as a dedicated mother and volunteer.

Mechele Linehan was hauled into court in Thurston County, Washington, and charged with murder. Her lawyer, Wayne Fricke, told the court that she would not fight extradition back to Alaska. Mechele Linehan, formerly Hughes, chose her defender well. Fricke described himself this way:

"As far as my background goes, I have been doing this [being a defense lawyer] for the last 22 years in both State and Federal courts. I have defended clients in a number of states out west, although primarily in the state of Washington. I defend clients charged with both white and blue collar crimes. I have been involved in numerous murder cases/ trials over the years. I think if you Googled my name you would get numerous hits in the local papers (i.e. Tacoma News Tribune, Seattle Times, Seattle P.I.), as well as other publications. You could get a pretty good idea of my background, as well as the types of cases I have been involved in over the years."

In the Linehan case, Fricke immediately told reporters, "We will put up a vigorous defense."

With bail set at $500,000 cash, Colin Linehan reached into his pocket, came up with it, plunked it down, and walked out of the courthouse holding his wife's hand.

"She's so strong and she's been through so much. She has resources inside of her. I know she will pull through. She's had a rough start in life," said a relative in an *Anchorage Daily News* story on the case.

On October 13, 2006, after being out of state for more than a decade, Mechele Hughes finally returned to Alaska as Mechele Linehan. With a newly appointed Alaska defense attorney Kevin Fitzgerald planning to ask the judge to reduce her bail from half a million to less than $100,000, there was a good possibility she could post bail and fly home to Olympia until her trial.

"There isn't any utility in having her in or out of jail in Anchorage," Fitzgerald was quoted publicly.

That morning, Mechele Hughes appeared in a Nesbitt County courthouse. She was wearing standard-issue mustard yellow prison overalls. She was cuffed to another prisoner. Colin Linehan was sitting in the courtroom's front row. Hughes looked over and smiled at Linehan many times. Whether Judge Larry D. Card noticed is hard to say.

Alaska attorney Larry D. Card was forty-five years old in 1993 when he made history, becoming Alaska's first African-American judge. A Kansas native, he had joined the air force. He came to Alaska in 1976 when he was twenty-eight years old. Specializing in defense work, Card rose to the rank of captain before leaving the air force to become a civilian criminal defense attorney who also did some civil work. That's what he was doing when he ascended to the bench.

Thirteen years later, Card was a veteran fifty-eight-year-old trial judge, denying the defense attempt to request a bail reduction. Instead, he put off a bail review until the following Monday. That meant that regardless of the coming proceedings, Mechele Hughes, aka Linehan, was behind bars . . . for the weekend. So Hughes availed herself of the state's facilities and promptly on Monday morning found herself before Judge Card again.

This time, defense attorney Kevin Fitzgerald passionately argued that his client was no danger to society, and that she was not likely to flee prosecution because she had a family. In turn, cold case squad prosecutor Pat Gullufsen—previously Juneau's district attorney—argued that the bail and custody proposals from the defense were more akin to those for a robbery suspect rather than a murder suspect.

Since it was a hearing and anyone with relevance to the case could testify, Fitzgerald called Colin Linehan to the stand. Linehan described his life with his wife in Olympia and went on to try and assure Card that he would actually call 911 if his wife "attempted to flee." Card not only didn't buy that argument, he also denied the bail review. Linehan was staying in Alaska at least for the near future . . . sort of.

On October 21, Card held court. It was obvious from his ruling that he had consulted the Eighth Amendment to the U.S. Constitution, which reads: "Excessive bail shall not be required, nor excessive fines imposed, nor cruel and unusual punishments inflicted."

Judges can do anything. They bring a lifetime of judgment and in some cases compassion to every ruling. Judge Card reduced Linehan's bail from $500,000 to $150,000 in cash, which Colin Linehan put up in cash immediately. He wasn't a millionaire and neither was his wife. But he could afford the $150K. If Judge Card had erred and she jumped bail, he would have erred on the side of the Constitution. But he also showed common sense in his ruling.

Mechele Linehan would be allowed to go back to Olympia all right, and live her life as a soccer mom until trial. However, unlike her fellow soccer moms, her ankle bracelet would be a tamper-resistant ankle monitor. With movements monitored through the use of radio frequency or GPS signal, her monitor would tell police quickly if she moved outside Olympia's confines.

In his ruling, Judge Card said that since Dr. Linehan and a coworker testified during the bail hearing that they would guarantee to watch her, they faced imprisonment if she fled prosecution and they didn't call the authorities posthaste. And then Mechele Linehan was freed to go home to Olympia, pending trial.

Kenneth Leppink's comment back in Shelby, Michigan, was "Through all this, my son seems to have been forgotten and the accused has taken the limelight as if nothing has ever happened."

The cases of John Carlin III and Mechele Hughes, aka Linehan, were different and would be prosecuted separately. It was a good decision on the part of the prosecution. It upped their chances of conviction in each case by 50 percent. A conviction against one could be used against the other.

Saying that the person who planned the murder is just as responsible as the person who pulled the trigger is one thing, proving it at trial is a whole other tender of fish. The farther away you get from the actual person who fired the shot, the farther away you get from conviction. It was therefore easier, in theory, to get a conviction on Carlin, the prosecution's alleged triggerman, than Hughes, aka Linehan, whom they alleged planned it out.

According to the theory, the conviction against Carlin could then be used against Linehan, making the still largely circumstantial case against her that much stronger. But if a trial judge can change his mind upon consulting United States history, a jury can change its collective mind on a whim and a wish. Or it could do its job, hear the evidence, and present a just verdict.

No matter how strong or weak the case is, every trial lawyer knows that going to trial is the ultimate crapshoot.

The trial against John Carlin III for killing Kent Leppink began in an Anchorage, Alaska, courtroom on March 14, 2007.

Part of the prosecution's case against Carlin lay in the ability of the big bearded guy at the defense table to get so sucked into a relationship with a stripper, he would do anything for her, including murder. In order to show that, the prosecution had to lay the groundwork of a pattern of narcissistic and predatory behavior by Hughes on Carlin III. That then led him to murder Kent Leppink.

To say it's a long way from "here" to "there," the latter being a murder conviction, is putting it mildly. For every case that goes to trial, there are nine others that have been settled with plea bargains. Only the cases where such a bargain cannot be sealed, or a high-profile murder case, wind up going to trial.

The reason for pretrial plea bargaining is simple. No matter the hard evidence, no one knows what a jury will do at trial. Prosecutors know that circumstantial evidence always makes it harder to get a conviction. So do defense attorneys, and Carlin had two good ones in Marcy McDannel and Sidney Billingslea. Gullufsen represented the state. The judge was Philip Volland.

Gullufsen approached the first witness for the prosecution, deputy chief medical examiner Norman Thompson. Eleven years earlier, he had been the man who conducted Kent Leppink's autopsy. His testimony was, to say the least, enlightening.

According to Thompson, *all three shots*—the ones to the back, stomach, and face—were fired *at close range*. Not only that, the gun was touching or within an inch of Leppink's skin when the killer fired the first bullet. That left the implication that this was a very personal killing. Otherwise, why get up so close?

During the give-and-take of direct and cross-examination, both sides seemed intent on establishing the time of death. It was particularly important to the defense because if they could show their client was someplace else when Leppink died, then he was innocent. Addressing this issue, Thompson testified about how hard it was to narrow the time of death into a much more specific window because rigor mortis had been affected by atmospheric conditions.

"At the very minimum, one would expect [time of death] 12 hours prior to the first time the rigor mortis was checked for. At the very minimum, at least 12 hours prior to that so say 4 A.M. of the 2nd would be possible. I'm skeptical because of the temperatures involved.

"What's important about this is that remembering that there's a hole in the skin and that blood from inside the body tends to leak out of, ah, bullet holes, there is no significant amount of blood leaking out of the hole to transfer itself to the T-shirt."

The jury ate it up. It was *CSI* time and they sat transfixed at Thompson's testimony. Next, Gullufsen called Rebecca Douglas, a cook at a restaurant in Hope, to the stand. Under direct examination, she told the jury that Kent Leppink had come into her restaurant days before he was murdered.

"He had come in too, looking for his girlfriend at the café," Douglas testified. "He showed me a picture of himself with a girl, and he wanted to know if I'd seen her in Hope."

Douglas's memory seemed to fade later during cross examination, when she admitted that she wasn't actually certain when Leppink had come into her café. It was possible it was actually two or three weeks before he was killed.

As Douglas left the courtroom, she heard Gullufsen announce behind her, "The state calls John Carlin the Fourth."

The sixty-one-year-old prosecutor, who had not been on the Alaska cold case squad for very long, waited patiently for the witness to take the stand. Having been admitted to the Alaska bar in 1974, Gullufsen served as an assistant attorney general in the government affairs section in Juneau from 1992 to 2001. Then he moved up the ladder rapidly in the rough-and-tumble world of Alaska politics.

In May 2002, Attorney General Bruce Boelho named Gullufsen to head the Criminal Division of the Department of Law. Gullufsen replaced Cynthia Cooper, the former deputy attorney general in charge of the Criminal Division. She had resigned "following two controversial cases and criticism of her office by a state judge and a federal judge," the *Anchorage Daily News* reported.

The following year, Gullufsen became Juneau's district attorney. He held that office until June 2006 when deputy attorney general Susan Parkes, who supervises the Department of Law's Criminal Division, appointed him a senior statewide prosecutor. "Pat's extensive experience in prosecutions makes him extremely well-suited to advise on our most challenging cases, including our cold case prosecutions," said Parkes at the time.

It was a very good choice and modeled on what had worked in other states—put an experienced criminal prosecutor with a high rate of convictions like Gullufsen on a cold case prosecution and you had a better chance of a positive result, especially when it was built on mostly circumstantial evidence. That was bad news for the killers of Kent Leppink, facing a relentless prosecutor who would not stop at anything except the truth.

John Carlin IV, a somewhat overweight twenty-seven-year-old, came forward and took the oath. He then settled uncomfortably into the witness chair.

"Could you tell us where you live?" Gullufsen began his direct examination.

"I live in Seattle, Washington," Carlin IV answered quickly.

"What do you do there?"

"I work for MacDonald Miller."

MacDonald Miller was a construction firm on Detroit Avenue in Seattle. "Delivering what we say we'll deliver, when we say we'll deliver it," according to their Web site.

"And how long have you lived in Washington State?" Gullufsen wondered.

"Four years."

"Do you remember living in Alaska?"

"I do remember living in Alaska."

Gullufsen went over to the defense table and picked up a box. He asked to enter it into evidence; the judge agreed.

"You recognize this?" Gullufsen asked, holding it up for the witness to see.

"I recognize the wood box. I owned it and kept items in it."

"Like what?"

"I collected shell casings. I may have had firecrackers in that box, photos, nothing important [in it]."

"Who is John Carlin III?"

"John Carlin III is my father."

The witness went on to briefly relate his family history.

"I went to Service High School in New Jersey. We come from New Jersey and technically I have family there. My mother was ill and we originally came up for vacation."

"When did your mother die?"

"My mother passed away in April of 1995."

"What happened then?"

"My dad purchased a new house and we moved into it."

Carlin IV found the attendance policies in his Anchorage high school a bit too restrictive. By 1996, he had to leave school because he kept skipping classes.

"I was not going to school at all," he related to the jury.

That wasn't too surprising. At the time Carlin IV went to school in Alaska, the school system was ranked twenty-fifth in the nation, while New Jersey's was fourth. By 2008, Alaska had moved down the Morgan Quitno state education system rankings list to forty-sixth position.

"Tell me about Mechele Hughes," Gullufsen asked.

"She lived in the house until we moved," with Kent who was referred to as TT by one and all.

"Do you remember Scott Hilke?"

"He never lived at our house."

"How about Mechele Hughes's house in Wasilla?"

"I have never been to the house in Wasilla prior to her living with us. When she moved, I did go to the Wasilla house. It was being worked on."

Carlin IV then explained how Carlin III had then collected a lot of money on the lead exposure lawsuit in 1996, the implication being this was how he had paid for the home repairs.

"All right, I show you," Gullufsen said, reaching for the Desert Eagle, which lay on the prosecution table, "this weapon. Can you identify it?"

While the murder weapon was not recovered, Gullufsen was using another Desert Eagle as an example. Carlin IV proceeded to identify the weapon.

"Yes, I remember my father purchasing a firearm from a newspaper ad."

"Was there something else that came with the weapon?"

"Yes, the case and holster were with the gun when it was purchased."

Introducing a gun holster as an exhibit, Gullufsen asked the witness to identify it. Carlin IV said that it was the holster that went with the gun, though he never actually saw the weapon itself holstered.

"Do you remember when Mr. Leppink died?"

"I do recall learning that Mr. Leppink was dead."

"All right, what else do you recall?"

"I do remember coming into the house and seeing Mechele and my father in the bathroom."

"The bathroom?"

"I remember seeing the gun in the sink."

It's like putting your hand into an electric socket and feeling that tingling all through your body. That's the best way to describe it when a witness suddenly says something of great relevance. Whether on the jury, at the defense or prosecution tables, or sitting in the public benches taking advantage of our public trial system, everyone is raised out of his courtroom torpor.

"What else do you remember?"

"I remember my father and Mechele—the gun in the sink and there was clear liquid in the sink and I smelled bleach. I don't think they expected me home." Carlin IV added, "I think there was a look of surprise."

No doubt, especially if you were trying to bleach a gun free of fingerprints, DNA, and anything else that bleach kills, which is just about everything. Not an easy to forget smell and everyone on the jury knew it. Now Gullufsen needed to be sure that the jury understood that the twenty-seven-year-old knew that his identification of the murder weapon was correct.

"You understand the difference between an automatic pistol and a revolver?"

"An [automatic] pistol has a magazine while a revolver has a revolving cylinder."

Carlin IV sounded like an expert.

"So you're sure of what you have seen?"

"I saw a pistol in the sink."

"Ever see it again?"

"I never saw it again," Carlin IV confirmed.

"Are you aware of the Desert Eagle pistol?" Gullufsen asked, trying to get even more specific with the witness's identification.

"I don't know off-hand what a Desert Eagle is. So I can't say one way or another whether it was a Desert Eagle."

To be expected. Neither did most people since the gun was so rare.

"What about the relationship between your father and Ms. Hughes?"

"Yes. My father and Ms. Hughes told me they were getting married."

"Had they traveled together?"

"I remember my father and Ms. Hughes went to Europe.

My grandparents came from New Jersey to stay with me and Rosco, my dog."

"Did Ms. Hughes have animals?"

"Ms. Hughes had three or four dogs, a couple of birds and a cat."

Then Gullufsen deftly turned the page back to Kent Leppink.

"What was their relationship like, Ms. Hughes and Mr. Leppink?"

"He seemed to be an errand boy. He seemed to iron a lot and he would iron a lot of things," Carlin IV testified.

That was because Leppink was neat. Had he worked in a dry cleaning store, he would have been the "presser," the worker who takes the clothing that has been dry-cleaned and flattens it out with a huge pressing machine. That's something Leppink would have liked.

Carlin IV testified that he knew Hughes was a stripper at the Bush but that he had never been there himself. He was, after all, seventeen years old at the time.

"Do you remember Mr. Leppink having a computer?"

"I do remember that. Mr. Leppink had a laptop computer. I did some school papers on it. I played computer games with him. Lots of card games and golf."

"Can you describe the last time you saw Mr. Leppink?" Gullufsen said, loud enough for all to hear even in the courtroom's back rows.

"The last time I saw Mr. Leppink, it was in the evening and I was going to bed. He was with my father. I was at the Wasilla house cleaning and remember when the police came and told us Mr. Leppink was dead."

"Where were you at the time?"

"In the storage shed. Emptying it out. It was a mix of his belongings and Mechele's belongings."

Implication, ladies and gentlemen of the jury: Carlin and Hughes were deliberately destroying evidence that might in any way connect them to the Leppink homicide. They were doing this before the cops officially told them their good friend had been brutally shot dead.

CHAPTER

11

Gullufsen took Carlin IV quickly through the purchase of the motor home that the young man and Mechele had left town in during the middle of the murder investigation. After describing their scenic itinerary through Sacramento—where they picked up a sofa at Scott Hilke's place—San Diego, and New Mexico, Carlin IV said they finally arrived in Hughes's hometown of New Orleans.

"We stayed in New Orleans a week," Carlin IV continued. Then he left. Maybe he didn't like being below sea level? "I had a cousin that was getting married in New Jersey. I flew back to New Jersey and stayed with my grandparents."

After that, his father came home.

"We moved back into the house we had in New Jersey."

"Home" was Elmer, in rural southern New Jersey. Rural southern New Jersey was a nice place to get lost in.

Gullufsen had already established where Carlin III had been for the last ten years. It was the man's nature that the jury needed to know about. Gullufsen wanted to know what John Carlin III was like.

"Can you describe your relationship with your father?" Gullufsen asked.

"My father and I got along well at times; and others, we did argue."

He said, "I would describe my father as a private person. He did not like to divulge personal information. As I recall, being informed we were going to New Orleans was sudden."

Was there a gun in the house, Gullufsen wondered aloud.

"I remember there being a gun kept in the pantry of the house. I believe it was a pistol."

The pantry? Considering that Carlin III was a baby boomer, he might have stolen the idea from TV private eye Jim Rockford, who kept his .38 in a cookie jar in the pantry.

Gullufsen then led the witness forward from the late 1990s to the present, how Mechele Hughes became Mechele Linehan, Washington soccer mom and devoted army wife. Like just about every person in the service, Dr. Colin Linehan had been dispatched into the Iraq War zone.

"Did you visit Mechele in Washington?" Gullufsen asked.

"I stayed with Mechele when her husband went to Iraq," Carlin IV answered. "When she would be out, I would be baby-sitting. Her daughter was four or five years old." As for visitors during the time he was there, "I don't remember Mr. Hilke being in the house but I do remember him stopping by."

If her past behavior is anything to go on, she was likely having an affair while her husband was in harm's way. The picture Gullufsen was painting of Mechele Hughes, aka Linehan, made the femme fatales in *Double Indemnity* and *The Last Seduction* look like pussycats in comparison. Life was surpassing art.

"No further questions," said Gullufsen.

After a thirty-minute recess Sandy Billingslea rose for the

cross-examination. She took Carlin IV through his relationship with Leppink.

"I was 17 and I don't remember how old he [Kent] was. I thought of him as an adult but did not think of him as an old person."

Pursuing the angle that Kent Leppink was a closeted gay man, Billingslea asked a question regarding any physical contact Leppink might have had with seventeen-year-old Carlin IV. The twenty-seven-year-old version then said crisp and clear:

"There was one time he did something that was uncomfortable. He made sexual contact with me. I told my dad about that. I don't remember my dad taking him aside and telling him not to do that."

It was a classic defense strategy. In some places, and with some juries, a gay man's life is not held in as high esteem as that of one who is straight. If you can put the decedent on trial, it takes attention away from the defendant and sometimes yields a not guilty verdict. Billingslea then established that the Wasilla home had four bedrooms and that "Scott sometimes stayed at our house, but when he was there, I didn't know where he slept."

Billingslea then turned to the time Carlin IV stayed with Hughes in Olympia, Washington, her new "hometown."

"Yes, I remember Mechele, when I was living with her in 2004; she went to Minneapolis to see him [Scott Hilke]. My understanding was they were friends."

But under patient questioning Carlin IV finally admitted, "I presumed at one point there was a sexual relationship between Mr. Hilke and Mechele."

That might imply to the jury that Hilke, not Carlin III, was Hughes's lover.

Going back in time again to Wasilla: "There were times when we were all at the house," Carlin IV stated. "TT and

Scott seemed very friendly to me, I never saw any harsh words between them. But Scott was not around a lot. When he was there, he would stay for maybe one night."

But it was Leppink who really seemed to be in love with Mechele.

"TT was very enamored of her; he had a crush on her. He would follow her like a little puppy—very evident. I think Mechele humored him but at times, she was annoyed by it. She would gripe and make fun of him. Mechele never gave me the impression she was going to marry TT."

As for what their future held together: "Mr. Leppink led me to believe he was going to marry her. He never showed me a ring. I never personally witnessed him buying her fur coats."

"Did he pay the rent on the house?"

"I don't know if Mr. Leppink paid the rent on the Wasilla house," he said.

"When did you first meet Mechele?"

"In November 1995, shortly before Thanksgiving. She spent Thanksgiving with us. It was not too long after my mom died that I went with my dad to shoot targets. That was before I met Mechele."

"What was it like when Mechele was home?"

"In Anchorage, she would come home with big bags of money and shake them out on the table [from stripping]. We all took care of her pets. Rosco and her cat and a couple of birds came with us in the motor home. This fellow in San Diego was a toucan expert—she had a toucan and she wanted to see about having it mated. I remember her talking about Costa Rica. Don't know what her plans were.

"My dad and Mechele took me in their rooms and told me they were going to get married. I was under the impression Mechele and Scott were broken up for awhile. I assumed they were having a sexual relationship when they told me they were getting married. TT was still living there."

"Did he say anything about marrying Mechele?"

"He had mentioned his intention of marrying Mechele."

All that changed, of course, after Kent Leppink's murder and the police came calling. The real question was why the teen never mentioned anything besides the gun.

"My dad was with me because I was 17 when the police came and spoke with me. I did not mention anything about the gun when I was in Louisiana and the police spoke to me [either]," Carlin IV explained.

Billingslea was showing Carlin IV to have been a conflicted teenager caught between telling the truth and ratting on his father. As to where Mechele Hughes wound up after all this, "She then moved to Olympia, Washington. My father told me she did."

"When was the last time you talked to Mechele?" the defense attorney asked.

"I have not talked to Mechele for three years. Sometime around the end of October 2004. When I left her house in Olympia, we had a falling out and never talked after that. We had a conflict of opinion about what I was doing and I did not think she was paying me enough [for his services]."

It seemed that Mechele Linehan had called the cops on "some tradesmen that had stolen some things from her. There was a dispute about not being compensated for some work they had done. She was mad at these guys, pretty agitated by it, cursing."

He said, "With me, it was more of a decision to get up and go. At times I was frustrated with not being paid. She was giving me room and board and [she] was supposed to pay me for the work I did," with her daughter and around the house.

"She stole my dog," he added. "I had to fly back to New Jersey. She kept Rosco and would not give him back. Long story short, I never got Rosco back."

After a three-minute conference in which the attorneys all crowded around the judge at the bench to discuss his next piece of testimony, Carlin IV was allowed to continue.

Years later in 2004, "Just out of the blue, I received an e-mail from her. My roommate and I had planned on moving to Washington." Hughes offered him a job and he took it. "It was a good opportunity for me to move. Emotionally, I was closer to Mechele. She was protective of me."

The implication seemed to be that during that time in Alaska, and afterward on the road and in New Orleans, he was emotionally closer to Mechele than he was to his father. When Carlin IV linked up with her again a few years later, he was an adult. Mechele was very candid about her sexual life in Washington State.

"I never witnessed them having an affair but she would tell me about the other doctor," who she was having an affair with while her husband was over in Iraq.

Even after he left Washington, Mechele Hughes got involved with him one more time, indirectly.

"In May 2005, Ms. Branchflower [from the cold case squad] came to talk to me. That was the first time I talked about my dad having a gun."

Billingslea wanted to know if he had made a deal with the prosecution for his testimony.

"Yes, I have been told I am not going to be prosecuted. Mr. Gullufsen did tell me I would not be prosecuted."

It was standard operating procedure to try to impeach the testimony of a state witness who had made a deal. Make it seem like he might lie in order to avoid prosecution for his part in a murder plot. Experienced prosecutors know defense attorneys are going to do this and so, on redirect, Gullufsen got to his feet.

"Has anyone put any sort of pressure on you to testify here today?" he pointedly asked.

"No one has put any pressure on me for testifying," Carlin IV answered.

"No further questions your honor."

The judge looked over at the defense; they had nothing more.

"Witness excused."

Carlin IV quickly left the witness box and the courtroom, having given the jury a lot to think about. After a break, Gullufsen got down to business. It was time to establish, in evidence, the Desert Eagle being the murder weapon, despite the fact that he didn't have it in person, evidence, or any which way. But there was a way to do it.

"The state calls David Michael Stilchen."

The man who took the stand had the rank and bearing of a military officer, which he was. After identifying himself for the record, Stilchen testified that he was active duty in the air force, and that he lived in Phoenix, Arizona. Previously, he had been in Anchorage. "Did you ever own a .44 caliber Desert Eagle?" Gullufsen suddenly asked.

"I did own a .44 caliber Desert Eagle," the air force officer concurred.

"Where'd you get it?"

"I purchased the gun from a friend that I was stationed with in Elmendorf [Germany]."

The gun he purchased, though, had some problems firing.

"I did have some work done on the gun because when it fired, it would stick. I did not fire it a lot after the gun was repaired. I was gone for five months and had it stored in storage. I decided to sell the gun when I came back from

Florida. When I returned back, I took my weapons out of the armory. I had moved off base and decided to sell the gun. So I placed an in the newspaper."

Gullufsen showed him the advertisement that Branchflower had found in the newspaper. Stilchen identified it was the ad he placed in the paper to sell his .44 Magnum Desert Eagle.

"That was my cell phone [number] in the ad," Stilchen said, by way of positive identification.

Direct evidence. Preston Wade was watching from the back of the courtroom.

Regarding the ad, "I believe [Mr. Carlin] was the first person I spoke to. I remember getting a phone call and I went over to the person's house. We made idle conversation, what he wanted the gun for. He gave me cash and I sold the weapon. I believe it was about $650 in large bills."

"Did he look at the weapon at all?" the prosecutor wondered.

"He did check out the weapon," Stilchen confirmed. "He dry fired it. He did not have any issues with firing it," though firing a gun "dry" can loosen the firing pen. Stilchen identified the case to his gun, the one confiscated from Carlin's residence.

"There was also a cleaning kit I don't see there," he also pointed out.

As for the gun, "This case was large because I kept two guns and other items in there. But I remember the [other] distinctly. I had a .22 caliber pistol" and the Desert Eagle. "My brother and I went several times to the gun range and that is where the weapon [the Desert Eagle] jammed."

The prosecutor produced a Desert Eagle, just like the one used in the murder. Stilchen demonstrated the problem he'd run into by pulling back on the slide.

"This is very similar to the Desert Eagle that I sold. The magazine is also very similar to the real one."

Gullufsen wanted to know when he had actually sold the gun to Carlin III and where.

"When I showed up to the house, it was night time. Nice house—very clean, everything seemed new."

Of course it was. Kent Leppink and John Carlin had paid for all the improvements.

"There was this large built-in wall unit," Stilchen continued. "It stood out in my mind because I had not seen [one like] that before. I had never been in a house that nice before and it stuck in my mind."

When he met Carlin III, Carlin had a specific reason for wanting the gun, or so he said.

"He indicated that he had recently moved to Alaska and wanted something that would drop a bear."

If it would drop a bear, it would certainly drop a human being. Gullufsen couldn't say it, but the statement hung in the courtroom air as it was.

"No further questions."

On cross-examination, McDannel took over for the defense. Her first question had to do with how Stilchen got involved actively in the cold case.

"The first time, I was contacted was by a female detective—Detective Branchflower," a member of the Alaskan cold case squad. Had she or anyone else showed him photos of Carlin or anyone else?

"I never received a photo of the person she was asking who I sold the gun to," the serviceman answered. "I never received any photographic line-up to look at."

This was very important. In most instances, a detective will ask a witness to identify a suspect through a "throw down"—a series of photographs literally thrown down on table in front of the witness. One contains the real bad guy, the other just mug shots of others. The hope is that the witness can look at the throw down and positively ID the suspect. In this case, for some reason, Branchflower had not used the throw down, relying on other information for identifying Carlin III as the buyer of the gun.

"I believe I told her he had dark hair," Stilchen continued, recalling events as best he could of a decade ago. "I don't recall if I said the gentleman was married and had kids or not. I did not go anywhere in the house—looked very clean to me."

"Did it have cathedral ceilings?"

"I don't recall if it had cathedral ceilings. I just looked at the wall unit and pretty much stayed focused on the kitchen. Only thing I recall was a couch, wall unit and TV."

As for a description of Carlin III at the time, "He was larger than I was and I am 6 feet. He was heavier than I was at the time. He had his shirt off when I came over. Burly is the best I can do."

On redirect Gullufsen asked about the man's age.

"My recollection at the time that he was in his late 30's or 40's."

"No further questions," and with no redirect from the defense, the judge announced, "Witness excused. We will break a little early today."

It was 1:05 P.M. The next day of the trial began with the swearing in of a new prosecution witness, Detective Preston Wade. He related the investigation of Carlin III and Hughes in connection with the Kent Leppink homicide. On cross-examination, the defense dug into a hole so big in the prosecution's case, you could drive a Dodge Omni through it.

"Did you take possession of Kent Leppink's Dodge Omni?"

"Yes, we did take and impound the Omni," Wade answered.

"What about searching it? You have a key to get in?"

"We did not search the Omni there." It was done later, at the station. "I don't remember if I needed a key to open the door."

Wade looked down at his notes.

"The passenger door was unlocked," he answered.

See, that was the mystery. If Leppink drove out to Hope and was ambushed there, how did his car get back to Hope? Unless of course there were two people on the scene when he was killed. Moving on to the search of Carlin's house, the defense attorney asked about how he happened to see the gun case.

"That gun case caught my notice," Wade testified. "It was there, out in the open."

"Would you say that it fit any particular kind of weapon?"

"It was not associated with any particular type of gun," Wade testified truthfully. "The room did not appear that it had a lot of stuff there. Some personal items. I went back there on June 6th with a search warrant.

"Things were packed up and it looked like people were moving."

"Where did you find the gun case?"

"The gun case was under the bedding."

Wade then went on to describe how Hope was a large geographical area, with a population "guessing a couple hundred." Reluctantly, he had to admit that when police went through the area with photos of Carlin III, "No one specifically recognized Mr. Carlin in the area."

"No more questions."

It was a bit of a rocky cross-examination. Perhaps it had succeeded in planting reasonable doubt in the minds of the jury that Carlin III was even in the area where Leppink as killed. Or the jury could just believe that Carlin III had simply avoided being seen, as a good murderer would. Looking over at the jury, there was no "tell," what gamblers describe as the giveaway gesture to what the opponent is thinking. The jury looked impassive.

Gullufsen got up for a bit of redirect.

"Was there any sort of identification from the people the state police talked to in the Hope area about seeing anyone who might have seemed out of place?"

"They may have said 'someone may have been here a couple weeks ago,'" the detective answered.

"Mr. Wade, are you familiar with the Desert Eagle?"

"I have handled a number of Desert Eagles."

Gullufsen showed him the gun case he had confiscated during the search.

"Take a look at it. Would that case fit a Desert Eagle?"

Wade carefully examined it and answered firmly, "That case would fit a Desert Eagle."

"No more questions," and neither did the defense have any more questions.

"Witness excused," intoned the judge.

CHAPTER

12

Jewelry or the presentation thereof by various suitors to Mechele Hughes was also part of the prosecution's case. That required the testimony of Sandy Pryor, the jeweler from 1996 who had sold jewelry to the whole menagerie.

"Could you state your name for the record?" the prosecutor began.

"Sandy Pryor."

"Good, now Ms. Pryor what do you do?"

"I'm a gemologist and I sell jewelry."

She went on to explain that she owned a jewelry store in the Anchorage area.

"Now did John Carlin III ever come into your store?"

"He came in and asked to look at a stone. Then he came in the following day and asked to purchase it."

"Can you tell us what 'it' was?"

"It was an $11,000 loose diamond."

The jury shifted collectively in their seats and more than one outtake of breath could be heard in the courtroom.

Carlin III sounded like he was loaded and wouldn't hesitate to spend it on a pretty girl like Mechele Hughes.

"Did Mr. Carlin explain what he was purchasing it for?"

"No he did not say what he was purchasing it for," the jeweler answered, repeating the prosecutor's words and then adding, "We set the stone in a platinum solitare ring."

"How much was it worth?" Gullufsen asked.

"Its appraised value," the jeweler answered slowly, "was $17,000."

"And did he say who this ring was for?"

"John Carlin said he purchased the ring for Mechele Hughes."

A few of the jurors turned to look at the defendant. Everyone else in the courtroom sat transfixed by Gullufsen's direct examination, except defense counsel, who objected a few times to various parts of the jeweler's testimony with no success.

"How long have you been in the jewelry business?" Gullufsen asked casually.

"Since 1974. I have sold a lot of engagement rings."

"Did you know Kent Leppink?"

"I did get to know Kent Leppink. Clients had brought him in and we became good friends."

"Did he come in and purchase jewelry?"

"He purchased jewelry for Mechele Hughes."

The prosecutor was again curious.

"What kind of jewelry? Could you be more specific?"

"An opal and diamond set. The retail cost was about $500. Kent also looked at the one carat flawless diamond as an engagement ring for Mechele."

She then went on to relate how Hughes had not been satisfied with the presents and had subsequently come in to exchange them.

"She brought the set back and a credit was given to him,"

meaning Leppink's account. Then, still another curious thing happened. The peripatetic Hughes called Pryor once again, from the road.

"When did Mechele Hughes next call you?"

"She spoke to me on April 30, 1996, and said she wanted a necklace. She was calling from Nevada about 3:00 or 4:00 in the afternoon. I ordered the necklace for her."

"Did she call again?"

"Yes, on May 6." Four days after Kent's body was found. "She said she wanted to use [Kent's] credit. I told her it was something we would have to discuss because it was Kent's credit."

"Now let me ask you about appraisals. How are they done?"

"If there is an appraisal request, the majority are done for insurance purposes."

Someplace, the dogged insurance investigator with the "little man in my stomach," was stirring.

"So the appraisal would still be done *for somebody*?"

"The appraisal would be in *someone's name*," the jeweler answered.

So who was it that asked for the appraisal? Pryor testified that the appraisal was done on jewelry owned by Mechele Hughes and put in her name but, "it was requested by John Carlin III."

That seemed to imply that they intended to get rid of jewelry Leppink had purchased for Hughes. Some juries might view that as getting rid of evidence.

McDannel rose to do the cross-examination of Sandy Pryor for the defense.

"So, Mr. Leppink ordered an opal and diamond set, a pendant with matching earrings retailing for about $500?"

"Yes."

"Was he by himself when he did that?"

"He was by himself."

"Then Mechele came in to exchange it?"

"Mechele comes in and says she wants a credit."

Later, "He came in and looked at a quarter carat diamond—he did buy that. That diamond was about the same price as the opal and diamond set. Mechele was with him when he bought it."

"Was Mechele with Mr. Leppink a lot?"

"They were definitely a couple. She would be hugging him, touching him, talking to him."

"Did Mr. Carlin come in with Ms. Hughes?" the lawyer asked.

"I believe Mr. Carlin and Mechele came in once or twice."

"And was she as friendly with Mr. Carlin as she was with Mr. Leppink?"

"I did not see any of the same type of behavior from her to Mr. Carlin."

In other words, the defense was suggesting that the very idea that Carlin could be in this woman's clutches like Leppink was out of the question. That would also make him resoundingly not guilty of murder since the whole prosecution case relied on believing Carlin was this woman's slave.

"Now Mechele or Ms. Hughes called you regarding an order for a chain and bracelet?"

"Mechele had called for a chain and matching bracelet."

"When was that?"

"April 30."

"What happened to the order after Kent was murdered?"

"I called her after Kent's death and she said, 'Apply Kent's credit.'"

So she did.

"Did she show any emotion about using her dead fiancé's credit to order a piece of jewelry for *herself*?" the prosecutor wondered.

"There was no shame or embarrassment on Mechele's part," Pryor answered, as if in confirmation that Mechele Hughes had no conscience, which was the whole point of the question.

No further questions, and McDannel sat back down. Gullufsen rose for the redirect.

"Ms. Pryor who purchased the diamond?"

"Mr. Carlin purchased the $11,000 diamond. Mr. Leppink had been looking at it shortly before."

"And the diamond was supposed to be part of what?"

"A ring."

"No further questions," and the witness was excused.

Finally, after ten years, the state had given a jury a direct piece of evidence—Carlin IV's testimony that Carlin III and Mechele Hughes were bleaching a gun. Unfortunately, the circumstantial evidence came in because the weapon had still not been recovered. But Carlin IV was positive that it had been an automatic, not a revolver, just as the prosecution was positive that it was an automatic and not a revolver that had been used to shoot Leppink. The jury could choose to believe that the dynamic duo were using bleach to wipe away every trace of fingerprints and DNA that would tie them to the crime, making them forensically aware killers.

Or the jury could choose to believe that the dynamic duo had found a new way of cleaning weapons they were going to patent in a new infomercial.

March 19

"The state calls Scott Hilke to the stand."

Handsome and sandy-haired, the third known former fiancé of Mechele Hughes came forward, took the oath, and settled in the witness box.

During questioning, he explained that it was he who was Hughes's first fiancé, having proposed to her in 1994. A traveling salesman for a company that manufactures steel valves, he thought he was her only true love. He had met Hughes as Bobbi Jo at the Bush and instantly fallen for her. Leppink and Carlin were saps who threw money at her to buy her affection.

He knew Leppink and Carlin III well, and upon reconsideration, he testified that Mechele Hughes had used and manipulated him like Carlin and Leppink and probably every other man in her life. "It became a very, very bad part of my life."

Hilke went on to describe how Hughes had introduced him to regular customers Leppink and Carlin at the Bush, where she made up to three grand a night between stripping and lap dances. Hughes introduced him to Carlin and Leppink at the club. He explained their complicated living arrangements, how everyone lived in Carlin III's house at one time or another immediately preceding Leppink's murder.

Whenever all three fiancés were there at the same time, Hilke said he was the one who slept with Hughes. The other two slept someplace else.

"Then what was Hughes doing with Carlin and Leppink?" Gullufsen asked.

"I think it was a dancer/client relationship that she was doing for economic purposes."

While not testifying to more specifics about what the men had bought her—probably because Hilke didn't really know—he then went on to recount a bizarre story about how he and Hughes had visited what the *Anchorage Daily News* reported as "a client's house for about an hour. The client had some affiliation with the mob, defense attorneys said. Judge Philip Volland stopped the line of questioning before the jury could hear further details."

That was a good move. Once the word "mob" was mentioned the jury's imagination could go to work. That, of course, was what the defense wanted. The jury could choose to believe that Leppink's death was some sort of mob whacking in return for who-knows-what. If that who-knows-what became reasonable doubt, Carlin would be acquitted. Never mind that the evidence did not indicate a mob killing. It would have been a lot neater, double tap to the head and it's over.

Hilke went on to testify that his engagement became a long-distance one. It was expensive commuting from Sacramento to Anchorage to see his fiancée, and eventually his money dwindled. After that, they saw each other over long weekends. He claimed that they "jetted" to different places, Hughes taking her exotic birds along for company.

The birds were an important part of Hughes's life. He claimed that Hughes told him that she had the money to finance a Costa Rican bird sanctuary project she was planning. This was right before Leppink's murder. During cross-examination, Hilke revealed that she also had a driver's license and passport in her sister Melissa's name though with her own photos.

No one disagreed that Hughes was behind the murder plot. But the defense needed to show that while it existed, their client was not part of it. It was to the defense's benefit to build up Hughes's level of deceit. At the same time, while it would have been nice to introduce Hilke as a likely suspect—fiancé number one jealous over fiancé number two—it was too difficult.

In court papers, Carlin's defense attorneys claimed that shortly after the murder, Hilke was given a lie detector test. The defense claimed in those papers that the result of the test showed that Hilke was giving "deceptive" answers. Alaska is enlightened enough not to accept lie detector tests as evidence in a criminal trial. There are so many factors that make lie detector tests unreliable, someone should write a book about it.

But the biggest bombshell of Hilke's testimony was that he and Hughes, now Linehan, had kept up contact *until 2005.* During that time, while Hughes was married to Dr. Linehan and Hilke to his wife, they cheated on their spouses and had a torrid affair.

The prosecution's theory of the crime, that Carlin was told by Hughes to whack Leppink, needed to be kept front and center for the jury. To help do this, Gullufsen called Mechele Linehan's older sister, Melissa, to the stand. Melissa, now using her maiden name, Hughes, was sworn in. With national media in the courtroom, she appeared particularly nervous. But that was understandable.

Melissa testified that immediately after Leppink's murder, her sister, Mechele, asked her to use her technical prowess to erase the files on a laptop computer that Mechele had taken from Leppink. Melissa refused. The prosecution introduced the incriminating e-mails recovered by their computer specialist, which showed in black and white the tangled love web that Mechele Hughes appeared to have woven to see Kent Leppink dead, with John Carlin as her assistant.

Melissa recounted her sister and Carlin IV's visit to her Utah home in 1997 and the confrontation over her refusal to erase the e-mails. In a subdued voice, Melissa testified that her sister didn't show any grief over the death of her fiancé.

"She said it was too bad 'someone didn't torture him first.' She told me that 'he got what he deserved. People didn't like him and he hunted and stuffed animals,'" Melissa testified, the last a reference to Leppink's background as hunter and taxidermist. The price for Melissa's honesty was that she and her sister did not speak for years.

When her testimony was over, Melissa Hughes broke

down in tears outside the courtroom. Back inside, Judge Volland had the jury removed to rule on a prosecution motion,
which of course the defense had objected to. Volland ruled
to allow a specific e-mail from Linehan to Carlin to be given
to the jury. Sent mere days before the murder, the e-mail
details how Carlin and Hughes were planning a move to the
Seychelles Islands in the Indian Ocean. The e-mail claimed
they couldn't be extradited from there to the United States
for murder.

Most murderers do not read history. Neither do some of the
reporters who reported on this account of the dynamic duo's
plan to flee extradition. If they did read history, they would
have found that a treaty has been in effect since 1932 with
the Seychelles. Ratified by the Senate on February 19, 1932,
signed it into law by President Herbert Hoover on March 3,
1932, it does allow extradition. Article 3 of the treaty says
that extradition shall be reciprocally granted for crimes or
offenses involving "Murder (including assassination, par-
ricide, infanticide, poisoning), or attempt or conspiracy to
murder; manslaughter."

Most murderers are also not as smart as they think.

It was now the defense's turn. The defense had decided to
use the O. J. Simpson defense: attack the investigation itself.
Their only two witnesses were an evidence technician and
one of the troopers involved in the original investigation. All
the while, Carlin in orange prison jumpsuit sat silent at the
defense table, no emotion crossing his face.

Neither of the two witnesses seemed to make much of
an impact. It had been a well-conducted investigation. The
jury, though, had to wonder—did Carlin himself have anything to say? The answer was no. In an apparent effort to
keep the spotlight turned away from him and back onto the
accused stripper killer whom much of the testimony had

been about, Carlin exercised his constitutional right not to speak in his own defense.

And the defense rested.

March 30

It was time for closing arguments in the state's case against John Carlin III. The state, as usual, went first. Gullufsen claimed Carlin was so obsessed with Linehan, he would kill for the stripper.

"Kent's death is what Mechele wants," Gullufsen said. "And John was willing to make it happen."

Again he showed the jury the e-mails in which Carlin and Hughes spoke of their love for each other, how they would deal with Leppink, and where they would go afterward. The insurance money was the motive, the prosecutor explained; Hughes would never marry Leppink. In fact, the murder had to occur sooner rather than later.

"Kent is getting to be problematic. He's getting to be snoopy and starting to look into things," Gullufsen told the jury of the time immediately preceding his homicide.

The idea was for Hughes to get Carlin to do the killing. She talked him into it, and then Carlin lured Leppink out to Hope where he killed him. Gullufsen opined that after luring him to the nonexistent cabin, Carlin pulled out the Desert Eagle and shot his friend three times at close range. He urged the jury to use their common sense in dealing with the evidence, be it direct or circumstantial.

Marcy McDannel rose to do the defense closing. Two photos in her hands, she approached the jury and stood directly in front of them. Then she raised the first photo of a particularly nasty-looking scorpion, and slapped it against a second photo of Mechele Linehan.

"People act consistent with their natures," defense lawyer

Marcy McDannel said. "She's the only one in this trial that has the nature capable of executing this cold-blooded, nasty act."

She maintained that the prosecution had not done their job. Their theory of the murder wasn't supported by the evidence. By immediately putting her client and Hughes out there as the prime suspects, they did not investigate others who might have been prime suspects as well.

Carlin and Leppink were friends, and Carlin had little reason to kill his friend. The defense version of the e-mails was simply empathy between two friends in the same romantic situation, nothing more.

"If there was a murder plot to kill him, why would they be talking so normally about future plans?" McDannel wondered aloud to the jury. "He [Carlin III] clearly has no knowledge of Mr. Leppink coming to an untimely end."

Attacking the prosecution's version of events, that the insurance money was the crime's prime motive, McDannel pointed out the large lawsuit Carlin had won in 1996. He didn't need money from any insurance policy; he had his own safely tucked in the bank.

In McDannel's version of events, it was an angry, out-of-control Hughes who shot the fisherman. She just couldn't take their relationship anymore. Murder was a way to easily end it, and make a few bucks for herself in the bargain.

She pointed out that while Carlin may have owned a Desert Eagle, the murder weapon was never found. *Direct evidence* was needed for a conviction. In the end, Carlin and Leppink had much in common.

"What does Carlin do for Mechele? He cleans up her messes," McDannel said, even perhaps helping her clean the weapon she used to kill Leppink with.

The summation concluded, Judge Volland charged the jury and they filed out to their deliberations.

* * *

On the afternoon of April 7, 2007, after a day and a half of deliberations, the Anchorage jury found John Carlin III guilty of the first-degree murder of Kent Leppink.

When the verdict was delivered, two jurors dabbed tears from their eyes. As he had during the trial, the orange-clad bearded man at the defense table showed no emotion. Carlin didn't even flinch. The judge postponed the sentencing until January and put Carlin in custody, for good.

"I'm dismayed to be quite frank," said defense attorney McDannel. "I feel the jury failed to grasp that there was just no proof of any—no real proof of any act that Mr. Carlin engaged in prior or during the murder of Mr. Leppink.

"If anyone was involved in this case, it was her [Hughes]. But now she can point her finger at John Carlin and she can say, 'He's been convicted of first-degree murder now. The jury concluded he was a killer what did I do? I was out of state.'"

Months later in January 2008 at his sentencing, Carlin said that he thought Leppink had planned out his own murder as a way to get back at the people around him he wanted to punish, specifically Carlin and Linehan. The convicted murderer questioned whether Leppink had done a last act of revenge by setting up the whole murder plot against the woman who had allegedly rejected him and the man she really loved. Carlin claimed to have protected Linehan by lying to Leppink about her whereabouts; that explained away the note.

Somehow, Judge Volland didn't buy it. Instead, he sentenced Carlin to ninety-nine years in jail.

"I'm pretty upset at the moment because I believe they have an innocent man in prison," said Carlin after the verdict was rendered and he was put behind bars.

"There's always going to be that part of me that realizes

that a big part of why he was found guilty was because of my testimony. And I know there were e-mails and other things like that. But in my heart, I know that's what did it. And I think that's the toughest part to live with," said his son.

As for Mechele Linehan, the verdict, and sentence, didn't appear to bother her. According to Wayne Fricke, her attorney, "She holds no ill will towards anyone. She is just worried about her case."

Maybe Hughes did indeed have something to worry about.

13

September 11, 2007

Point Pleasant in Brick Township, New Jersey is 4,383.35 miles from Anchorage, Alaska. It's a nice, pleasant seaside community, where Pat Giganti decided to settle after his relationship with Mechele Hughes broke up in the mid–1990s. He got married, had children, got into the building trade, and thought that relationship was well behind him.

Until he got a phone call. He hadn't heard from her in years. At first, Giganti was dumbfounded at the call, until Mechele Linehan started talking. Then all became clear.

"It was on the eve of the trial," Giganti remembers. "Mechele called me before the trial, right out of the blue. She asked me not to say anything about her to anyone. She was very concerned about what I might say," Giganti continued.

She was especially concerned that he might say something about the problems they had had in their relationship, like Giganti's earlier statement that "she took money off me." Linehan was tampering with a potential witness. If the prosecutor knew about it, he probably wouldn't have liked it very much. But Linehan need not have worried.

Neither the prosecution nor the defense had Giganti listed as a witness. It is even possible they didn't know he existed. Regardless, Giganti was not talking to anyone unless they called him first. The last thing he wanted was to get involved with his ex-lover. It had crossed his mind that if the charges against her were true, he could just as easily been the victim instead of Kent Leppink.

In court on the first day of the trial, Mechele Hughes looked like a dead ringer for Linda Fiorentino in *The Last Seduction*. Oh man did she, right down to the little smile, that little smile that said, "I know things that you don't." Seated at the defense table, she was dressed in a black suit that made her look like a prosperous businesswoman. On either side were her attorneys, including Wayne Fricke, a terrific defense attorney from Washington State that she had hired. Her husband, Dr. Linehan, sat behind her, a perpetual expression of concern on his unlined, handsome face.

At the prosecutor's table was Pat Gullufsen. The attorneys had already gone through voir dire, the simple question-and-answer process of potential jurors by prosecution and defense alike. They had chosen the jury of twelve, who Judge Philip Volland then seated. After some behind-the-scenes wrangling over the usual crap before a trial begins, Gullufsen finally rose on September 11, 2007, to deliver his opening statement. If Hughes wasn't worrying before, she might want to have checked the date.

Pat Gullufsen had a daunting problem. To prove guilt beyond reasonable doubt, he needed to symbolically put the Desert Eagle in Mechele Hughes's hands. Not after the crime, but before. That made it premeditated murder. He needed to show that Hughes/Linehan had a deliberate plan to commit a homicide.

The prosecution felt Mechele Linehan was the most conniving murderer they had ever seen. Unfortunately, she hardly looked like anyone's conception of a conniving stripper. With her dressed to the nines in black suit and white blouse, all it would take would be one out of twelve jurors thinking the smashingly gorgeous young woman with the jet black hair who sat at the defense table was:

A soccer mom.

Holder of a master's of public administration.

The wife, ladies and gentlemen of the jury, of a brave army doctor serving his country in Iraq, while she holds down the home front.

If you were betting going into Mechele Linehan's trial, what with all that going for her and seemingly little or no direct evidence linking her to the crime, a hung jury would be a most likely outcome. Surely one man on the jury would feel for her and vote not guilty. They always had. The defense would have easily taken a hung jury.

Sure a reprosecution would be possible, but maybe also a deal, and who knew, maybe the state would finally say they had too weak a case and throw out the charges. Or maybe frontier justice would prevail.

"Thank you for being patient with us, ladies and gentlemen," Judge Volland said before the testimony began. "Mr. Gullufsen, you have the floor," he said, as the court stenographer in the well of the courtroom began typing away.

Gullufsen rose.

"Thank you your honor. Counsel, may it please the court, good morning ladies and gentlemen," and he turned to directly address the jury who would decide whether Mechele Hughes finally walked for the murder of Kent Leppink, or spent the rest of her life behind bars for conspiring to do it. In the eyes of the law, conspiracy to commit murder was the same thing as pulling the trigger.

"John Carlin shot and killed Kent Leppink. I don't think there will be any dispute about that. If we are going to dispute that, we'll put on the evidence that supports that. As you saw in your jury questionnaire, he's been tried and convicted for that, but, if it wasn't for Mechele Linehan[,] Kent Leppink would still be alive today because she set the stage and she at least wrote the ending."

Kenneth and Betsy Leppink listened in the courtroom stoically.

"All she needed was somebody to help her fill in the blanks, somebody to do the dirty work, somebody to pull the trigger, and she found an able and willing partner in John Carlin III. Now I'd like to focus on two dates here a little bit and talk about them. April 1, 1996 and May 2, 1996."

Cold case time.

"On April 1, 1996, Mechele, then Hughes, walked into the New York Life Insurance Company offices here in Anchorage and she gave them a check for $2,600. It paid the premium on a million-dollar life insurance policy on Kent Leppink and a $150,000 life insurance policy on herself. That check was written on her own account. She paid the premium on those policies and shortly after that she left Anchorage and went south to Louisiana, to New Orleans."

It was important to introduce the Big Easy early because so much of what happened in the case revolved around Hughes's movements to and from New Orleans. The jury needed to understand her peripatetic lifestyle, not to mention her interesting living arrangements.

"She had only been in town at that point, back in town after being gone for a couple weeks, a couple of days, and the evidence will indicate that she had no other real purpose in being back here for those few days than to wrap up the insurance policy. Now you will hear great detail about the insurance policy and how it arose. What I believe the evidence is going to indicate is that it was set up this way."

Time to detail for the jury the murder plot as it unfolded.

"Back in March or February of 1996, Mechele Hughes agreed to set specific dates to marry Kent Leppink. Kent Leppink was overjoyed. That set the context in which Ms. Hughes was able to arrange to go in and start the process to obtain these life insurance policies. You'll hear testimony from the life insurance agent who was involved here, that it takes a period of time, particularly for a large policy like that.

"You have to go through an application process that includes a health check-up and some lab tests and it takes awhile, so that process started shortly after Ms. Hughes told Mr. Leppink that she indeed would marry him, and you'll all hear testimony that it was of significance now that there was a fiancé, a marriage relationship. Otherwise the ability to obtain a million-dollar life insurance policy on someone without that close connection was difficult, so that process was set in motion."

Ladies and gentlemen of the jury, read murder plot, with Mechele Hughes at the center of it.

"The only problem," Gullufsen continued, "you will hear about in that regard, the process really is that according to Lora Aspiotis, a then friend of Ms. Hughes, Kent insisted that they both get million-dollar insurance policies. That

made her mad. But what happened was they would not
insure her for a million dollars, so the only thing they would
insure her for was $150,000. Thus, on April 1 when the poli-
cies were ready and she paid for them, the $150,000 was
hers with Kent as beneficiary. The million-dollar policy was
still split like this: 80 per cent went to Mechele Hughes and
20 percent to Mr. Leppink's parents.

"Now there were some changes in that during the month
of April and we'll take a closer look at what the evidence
will be as to the month of April, because Kent began to look
into a few things. The evidence will indicate he began to
get suspicious and he looked into a few things," Gullufsen
repeated the phrase, probably deliberately.

"At one point in April he removed Mechele all together.
Shortly after that, he put her on as a 100 percent beneficiary
and then when she left town and he couldn't find her and he
believed that she had taken some things of his and believed
that she was involved romantically with Mr. Carlin, unbe-
knownst to her, he took her off altogether. That was on April
26, about five days before he was found dead.

"So that's April 1," he said, going back to his earlier comments about important dates in the case. "April 1 is the date
at which time if Mr. Leppink is to die, Ms. Hughes is going
to be the beneficiary of a large amount of money," $1 mil-
lion in life insurance dough.

"Now May 2. On May 2, 1996, this is Mr. Leppink. He's
very close to Hope, Alaska on a road off the highway that
leads to basically nowhere. There's an electrical facility on
one of the roads that you take, kind of a power line trail.
He's up it a short ways. You'll hear testimony about the exact
location, how far off the road and other circumstances surrounding the scene of the crime."

Had to get that phrase in.

"You'll notice that Mr. Leppink is on his back. That is

how he is found, you will hear testimony from Dr. Thompson the pathologist who conducted the autopsy, and you'll be able to put that together with the information received from troopers who were on the scene, and they will testify that Leppink was shot three times.

"Ultimately, he was shot with a Desert Eagle .44. This ladies and gentlemen," and Gullufsen picked up a pistol from the prosecution table to show the jury, "is a replica. It's not a real firearm. We will have a real Desert Eagle here for you as an exhibit in evidence, but this is a plastic weapon that shoots pellets."

He let the jury look at it.

"It's a big gun. The tracing of this weapon to Mr. Carlin was part of the case against him, and we may get into a little bit of that in this case, if we need to. But the manner in which he was killed according to the testimony you're going to hear basically was intermediate range from behind; he was shot in the back. He then most likely spun slightly around, fell down on the ground on his back. There's dirt on his pant that is suggestive of that. Then he was shot in the stomach and then he was shot in the face, the right side of the chin."

Gullufsen hadn't pulled any punches. He wasn't going to flinch from the facts. The jury needed to see how calculated, in the prosecutor's opinion, the whole thing was.

"He was not robbed. Nothing was taken from him. There's no indication he was placed there after death rather than shot right there and left there, but every indication is whoever shot him clearly wanted him to be dead and wasn't interested in taking anything from him.

"The pathologist will establish a range of time for his death, from six to eight to 36 hours prior to his being found."

That was a big hole the defense could exploit.

"He was found around 10:30 A.M. on the morning of May

2 by Chugach electrical workers who were there on the job. So according to Dr. Thompson the probable time of death is between late in the evening on April 30, 10:30 in there, to the very early morning hours, possibly May 2 within that range. Establishing anything more definite than that according to the pathologist just can't be done under these circumstances."

The circumstances were the cool Alaska temperatures that served to protect the body from decomposing more than it did, which seemed to be minimally. But that whole timeline of death the prosecution was presenting also meant that Mechele Hughes could have been at the scene of the crime at the time of death. The evidence showed that she had come back into town the night of the murder.

"Now one of the most important issues in this case is going to be how in the world—there was no car found that would have belonged to Mr. Leppink at the scene where he was found dead. One of the issues becomes how did he get there and why was he there. I want to get back to that, but first let me talk about the players in the case and how they all eventually connected together and then talk more about the significance of Mr. Leppink being found where he was."

Gullufsen went on to describe for the jury Leppink's relationship with Shirley and Russ Williams and how he came to command the *Togiak*.

"Now Kent Leppink is not a perfect person," Gullufsen continued. "He has the blemishes, and you will learn that there had been a problem about three, four, five years before that. The family owns a number of grocery stores in Michigan and Kent had stolen from those stores, and the family took care of it. Kent's interest in the business was revoked and he started another career. At that time—his nickname you will hear is 'T.T.'—he went to Tennessee and started to be a taxidermist for awhile, so Russ and Shirley Williams dubbed him T.T., 'Tennessee Taxidermist,' and that's what a whole lot of people called him."

Gullufsen continued to paint the portrait of how Leppink redeemed his life in Alaska. And like so many others before him, as Johnny Paycheck once sang, he was looking for love in all the wrong places.

"Kent began to frequent the Bush Company and in 1994 was probably the first time he saw Mechele Hughes at the Bush Company. As he put it, he immediately fell in love with her. He became obsessed and basically head-over-heels with Ms. Hughes. At some point in time in late '94, she had purchased a small house in Wasilla. Ms. Hughes continued to work at the Bush Company. Mr. Leppink would stay at the Wasilla house when he wasn't out in the summer in Prince William Sound tendering."

So far so good.

"Mr. Hilke was an industrial salesman who sold industrial valves who had come up to Anchorage I believe for the first time some time in '94. After the project he was working on here was done, he stayed around because he, too, has met Ms. Hughes and he, too, had fallen in love with her. They had actually become engaged sometime in late 1994, and were looking at the Thanksgiving of 1995 as a date to get married. So Mr. Hilke stayed at the Wasilla house. He wasn't working for most of the time he was there."

That meant while Leppink thought he was the only fiancé, he wasn't. Far from it.

"In the late fall of 1995, he [Hilke] starts working again on his occupation. He starts leaving town more. By the end of 1995, early 1996, he moves south again. He's from Sacramento, California, in that area. He basically moves back there and after that did not come back to Alaska. But he and Ms. Hughes, although they end up postponing their wedding date, remain romantically involved. As Ms. Hughes put it,

Mr. Hilke and her probably would have gotten married at some point."

Oh what a tangled web . . . no wonder the cops referred to it as "the black widow" case. "In late 1995, early 1996, Ms. Hughes became engaged to John Carlin III." That would make Carlin III officially fiancé number three.

"John Carlin III is from New Jersey, he had just moved to Anchorage in late 1994. He had reached a settlement in a lawsuit he had begun back there and had by early 1995 received a substantial sum of money somewhat in the area of $800,000 as a result of settling at least part of that lawsuit. He came to Anchorage with his young son, John Carlin IV who then was I believe 16, and a wife, who was terminally ill."

He left out the aurora borealis part. The last thing a prosecutor wants to do is paint a convicted murder as anything sympathetic, especially if you want to use *that* conviction against the person you believe started the whole murder plot in the first place.

"It was not long after they came to Anchorage in April of 1995 that she passed away. She was quite a bit older than Mr. Carlin. He had purchased a new house in Anchorage, January 21, 1995. Not long after that, he got here, they had decided to stay. He began to frequent the Bush Company in June 4 or thereabouts in 1995. He met Ms. Hughes and established a relationship with her and became infatuated with her."

The jury was forward in their seats, enraptured by Gullufsen's presentation.

"In August of 1995, he [Carlin] took Ms. Hughes to Europe with him. They had a three week trip to Europe. He began to buy her expensive things, and sometime in January—December of '95, January, maybe February of '96—they announced to John Carlin IV that they were engaged."

Fiancé number three.

"Mr. Carlin IV indicated he was 16 turning 17. He's just lost his mother and he's acting out a little bit, and somewhat of an issue, but not all that more than many teenagers about that age.

"Now in 1996 Mechele Linehan—well, actually, in November of 1995. She moves into Mr. Carlin's house. It's on Brook Hill Court south of the Anchorage area, towards Old Seward Highway. She moved there ostensibly because her house in Wasilla hadn't been ventilated right and it was rotting. She was able to move into Mr. Carlin's house where Mr. Carlin and his son were living.

"Sometime in January, Mr. Leppink, who had stayed up in the Wasilla house, also moved into the Brook Hill Court house and was staying there. In the meantime as I've indicated, Mr. Hilke had by that time early 1996 left Alaska, though he was in fairly frequent contact with Ms. Hughes, and Ms. Hughes traveled a lot. Using for the most part Mr. Hilke's mileage [from the airlines] she would fly down to see him fairly regularly, and during 1996, there are periods of time where she was gone for a couple for weeks at a time doing that or visiting relatives or family in New Orleans."

Then came a surprise.

"So that brings us to 1996 which I wanted to focus on a little bit. There's another individual whose name will come up, Jeff Fields. He lived and worked in Barrow, Alaska during this period of time '95/'96. He had also met Ms. Hughes at the Bush Company where she was employed. After Mr. Leppink's death and some months into the investigation, he told investigators, yes, he knew Ms. Hughes quite well and that she was his girlfriend and that she would be moving up to Barrow pretty soon. There was a red truck in Anchorage that was used whenever she basically wanted that he had left for her to use. When she needed money, she would call him in Barrow and receive money."

One thing about Mechele Hughes, Linehan, or whatever she called herself: she got around.

"So we enter 1996. Shortly into it, around February there was still some kind of marriage plan or something with Mr. Hilke. There's an engagement to Mr. Carlin and there's Mr. Leppink getting geared up for what he believes is a serious intention by Ms. Hughes to marry him, thus leading him to obtain life insurance for her as the substantial beneficiary. Also leading him to make out a will leaving her as his primary beneficiary which was signed on April 28, 1996 in Mr. Brundin's office, who was Mr. Leppink's attorney.

"But let's get back to Mr. Leppink being found in Hope. He had no connection with Hope. He had no business there, he had no friends there. He didn't know anybody there."

Then Gullufsen used an overhead projector to show the jury the Hope note that had lured Leppink to his death.

"The evidence will be that this note was left for Mr. Leppink to find on or around April 25, 1996. In the house in the bathroom. The evidence will demonstrate there was no cabin in Hope."

Sounded like the title of a bad novel.

"The evidence will demonstrate there was no cabin in Hope. That's a complete fabrication. Ms. Hughes actually after authoring that note with Mr. Carlin and leaving it for Mr. Leppink, flew to California to spend the weekend with Mr. Hilke at Lake Tahoe, and it is most likely before she got back from that trip that Mr. Leppink was found dead in Hope.

"The previous Saturday, the 27th, he had actually been in Hope looking for Mechele Linehan. He actually called his mother on the way to Hope to find her. The evidence will indicate he went down there over the weekend of the 27th/28th, could not find her, obviously because she was not there and there was no cabin there. But he remained convinced that she was there, still looked for her, and got down there at least one more time when he was killed where he was found."

Gullufsen then took the jury backward in time to April, when Leppink left Alaska to visit his parents and siblings in Florida.

"It's during this period of time that Mr. Carlin begins to get very, very vocal and adamant in his romantic feelings about Ms. Hughes. She begins to respond more directly in the emails to that, and what you're going to see in the emails, between her and Mr. Hilke, her and Mr. Carlin, and her and Mr. Leppink." Some had been deleted and the police couldn't recover them. "We'll talk a little bit more about that. Mr. Leppink is talking about marriage plans with Ms. Hughes. As soon as Mr. Leppink goes to Florida, he gets an email from Ms. Hughes demanding the $2,500 for a wedding dress that she says she has purchased in New Orleans and there's somewhat of a fight and email argument about spending the $2,500 on the wedding dress, but she demands to have it. She indicates she got her grandpa to spend the money on it and now he doesn't trust her, so she demands to have the $2,500."

Hughes, apparently, took no prisoners. If it was money she wanted, at least according to the prosecutor, she got it from whichever of her conquests she decided to pressure.

"You'll see evidence that Kent is getting pretty broke about this time. Mid April he borrows $10,000. By the end of April, that $10,000 is gone. It's spent on, I think, $1,500 to his attorney Mr. Brundin, well over $3,000 for cabinets for Ms. Hughes's Wasilla house, $31,000 cash directly to her, and some miscellaneous expenditure and then it's pretty much gone and he's back.

"One thing that becomes clear in the email exchanges while he's in Florida and she's in New Orleans is that after the fight Mr. Leppink has over the nature of the relationship, he apologizes all over himself for being argumentative with Ms. Hughes. He tells her that it's all his fault because he misled her and led her to believe that he had money and it was now time to budget, so she is learning directly, if she did not suspect it by now, that Kent doesn't have any money [of his own]. The only value he has, as the evidence will indicate, to Ms. Hughes is dead."

Gullufsen went on further with more details of the murder plot, how Leppink was killed (again), the police investigation, and the subsequent recovery of e-mails from Leppink's computer using modern forensic computer technology.

"And the 31st of March, in this email, Ms. Hughes indicates perhaps her real intentions or real attitude towards this marriage and that Kent is gearing up for," the prosecutor continued. "This is an email she writes to her mother. We believe the evidence will indicate that this email reveals her state of mind, which is that the whole marriage arrangement with Kent is a fabrication, and we believe that evidence will place this email in context where she is ridiculing the whole idea. This is right before she pays for the life insurance policy."

In other words, she was using him.

"Here's an email on the 12th from Ms. Hughes to Mr. Carlin. She appears to be concerned that he might be pulling away. Another one on the 16th to Mr. Carlin where she appears to be quoting from an earlier email by him, expressing that he is the most important thing in her life. Here is an email by Mr. Carlin," and he held it up, "expressing his deep feelings for her and how wonderful it makes him feel."

Then, quoting directly from the e-mail:

"I want to reiterate that I will never leave you, cheat on you, desire anyone else but you, and I'll worship the ground you walk on, the air you breathe, and the glow of your being. I love you forever."

It was a well-written heartfelt sentiment that was a prelude to murder by proxy. Gullufsen continued to make his point.

"The email on the 28th, it would appear she is saying 'What Did Kent say when you said I was 2 ½ hours away and he would have to come get me?' The evidence will indicate she's referring to the Hope area, but that her time estimate was a little off. And then she talks about, 'I love you very much, I miss you and I can't wait to go on our getaway. Did you know you can buy a citizenship in the Seychelles for around 10 mil no matter what crimes you have committed, they will not extradite? I found that out yesterday."

The judge had set a time limit for the openings, and the court informed Gullufsen he was running out of time.

"I thank you very much for your time. It's now the opportunity for the defense to provide their opening statement. At the end of the case, we think that some of the work the defense does in this case will be helpful to us all in understanding, finally, what happened and we look forward to hearing it.

"Thank you."

With that, Judge Volland took a fifteen-minute recess before the defense presented their opening statement.

14

M r. Fricke," said the judge, "you may proceed when
ready."

Wayne Fricke, Linehan's Washington State defense
lawyer who was commuting back and forth to Anchorage
during the entire trial, rose to address the court.

"Thank you your honor," he began. "Your honor if it may
please the court, Mr. Gullufsen, counsel and your colleagues,
Mr. Fitzgerald [her other attorney], Colin and Mechele, the
Leppink family and others, ladies and gentlemen.

"A lot of what you're going to hear is not going to be dis-
puted as far as it relates to who killed Kent Leppink. I'm
going to apologize right now if I mispronounce his name. It's
not intentional and I apologize to the family. I'm probably
going to refer to him as TT because it's easier for me, but
again we're not here to dispute who killed TT, and we agree
with Mr. Gullufsen here that in fact, it's John Carlin.

"Where we part ways is the suggestion that Mechele Linehan, then Mechele Hughes, is in any way responsible for his
death. In the last year, her life has turned upside down and

it's based on our belief, what the evidence will demonstrate, on nothing more than speculation and a gut feeling, that she was somehow potentially responsible for his death when he wrote that letter to his parents in 1996. We think he was right in one regard. He called it right when he felt that John Carlin III was going to shoot him, was going to kill him, but beyond that, there's not going to be evidence, not one bit of evidence that Mechele in any way wanted it to happen, asked that it happen, made any solicitation, made any plan or knew that it was going to happen or than she was even present.

"Based on that at the end of this case, we're going to ask that you find her not guilty on the evidence that both the prosecution is going to show you and that the defense is going to show you through a number of ways, whether it's documentation, the emails Mr. Gullufsen showed you, Mechele was not supposed to be aware of this situation and she wasn't. But I think it's important right now in general terms as to who Mechele Hughes is today, Mechele Linehan as who she is today."

He then went on to cite her new life in Washington State, complete with degree, husband, child, and baking cookies for neighbors.

"Now who she is today isn't meant to say she's perfect in any way. She comes from Louisiana. She didn't have a lot of money and she was seeking to make a living and ultimately what she did is become an exotic dancer and there's no dispute about that; she was doing that in New Orleans. After talking to some friends who advised her that perhaps she could make a better living in Alaska, she moved to Alaska and became employed at the Bush Company. When I say employed, I mean it's more like you're independent contractors."

An interesting way to describe taking your clothes off, gyrating down a pole, and showing every orifice of your body.

"Approximately in 1994, she buys the Wasilla house." Then she meets Scott Hilke at the Bush. "They strike up a relationship. They start dating, as we all start dating when we meet someone for the first time and ultimately, the dating gets serious and they fall in love with each other.

"In addition to that, she met TT, actually about a month prior. He's smitten with her, she's smitten with him, and also during this time, she's thinking about putting down some more firm roots in the Alaska area and purchasing the house. They met at the Bush, he was attracted to her and maybe even bought her a couple gifts at the time but again, there was no relationship."

Kent Leppink might have said otherwise were he alive.

"Conversely, she had a sexual relationship, romance, intimacy, with Scott Hilke and that intimacy is something that existed from early on in their relationship. She also meets John Carlin, Sr., who you've heard about; he's a big player in this case. He becomes smitten with her as well. They go on a trip in August of 1995. Mr. Carlin allows her to use the big black gun, which turns out to be the Desert Eagle, for a gun class where Mechele and several others want to get a concealed weapons permit."

There's a frightening thought.

"The interesting thing about all this is everybody knows about the relationships. TT knew of Scott Hilke, Scott Hilke knew of TT and when Mr. Carlin comes in the picture—and I would say he comes in the picture primarily when they move in together into his house. That brings them all together. Even when Scott Hilke is away, he stays at Carlin's residence.

"So that gives you a bit of background." As far TT was concerned, "I think the evidence is going to demonstrate as

Mr. Gullufsen said, that they're setting dates, pushing for dates, she's talking about dates he wants to get married right away and she's kind of pushing back. We don't dispute that. What she's trying to do as far as her relationships go, because her true love, quite frankly, is Scott Hilke. Now John Carlin Sr., has got stuff going on and he and TT have a relationship was well. He loves Mechele. He wants to possess her, and again there's no dispute as to that.

"There's one document I want to show you. I believe the evidence is going to show that this document was written after the murder on the laptop computer. It's written from John and he has a way—he always signs something with 'all the love, I have to give you.' In it, he says, 'I know that you'll be fine. I must just figure out what to do with my life. I have asked you what to do and you have said you don't know what to tell me. It is my problem that I have created and it is my responsibility to fix it. I must do that for me and John [IV].' And we suggest to you that in essence is a confession to the murder, of something apart from Ms. Linehan. He's had ample motive.

"Mr. Gullufsen indicated that John Carlin Jr. had indicated that in one of his recent statements in front of the grand jury, that when he came downstairs after the fact that there was this gun in the sink and it was being washed with bleach that Mechele and Carlin Sr. were there at the same time."

Fricke went on to say that this contradicted some of his previous statements to police officers.

"Based on the evidence, all of the evidence, Mr. Fitzgerald and I are going to ask you to find Ms. Linehan not guilty because there's no evidence to suggest that she was any part, any way involved in the murder of Kent Leppink. Thank you."

As Fricke sat down, the judge addressed the jury.

"Ladies and gentlemen, we're going to take another recess here before we begin testimony so we'll see you in 15 minutes."

Fifteen minutes later, Gullufsen began his case by putting the cops and pathologist on the stand to establish the cause of death and the length and breadth of the investigation. Carlin IV was called to the stand to repeat his testimony about bleaching the gun. Then Gullufsen called the one witness he felt could bring everything together and make it absolutely clear how the plot went down.

Gullufsen's intent was to show *The Last Seduction* in the courtroom. He hadn't emphasized the film and the plot during his opening, but now was the time. However, Judge Philip Volland had screened the film himself in chambers and didn't see enough similarities between it and the murder of Kent Leppink to justify entering it into evidence. He then said no to the prosecution request to introduce *The Last Seduction* as direct evidence and screen it for the jury. That didn't mean, of course, that Gullufsen couldn't reference the film. He just couldn't show it.

There had been a conference between the defense and prosecuting attorneys with the bench, regarding the testimony of the star witness for the prosecution. It had been held out of jury earshot to maintain a fair and balanced trial.

"Mr. Gullufsen."

"Thank you your honor. The State's next witness will be Lora Aspiotis. M'am, if you'd stand and approach the stand, the clerk will let you know what to do.

"M'am if you'd just go around the small wall and stand beside the witness chair please? And raise your right hand."

After doing what she was told, Aspiotis raised her right hand.

"Do you swear to tell the truth, the whole truth and nothing but the truth so help you God?"

"Yes," Aspiotis firmly answered.

"You may be seated," the clerk intoned.

Much like the stage manager in Thornton Wilder's *Our Town*, Gullufsen left the stage, in this case the well of the courtroom to let the action take place. Seated in his place near the judge, the clerk intoned in the best impression of Bob Sheppard, Yankee Stadium's long-time PA announcer:

"For the record, please state and spell both your first and last name."

"Lora Aspiotis. L-O-R-A, A-S-P-I-O-T-I-S."

"M'am you lived in Alaska at one time is that correct?" Gullufsen began his direct examination of the witness.

"That's correct."

"What was the period of time?"

"I moved here 1990 until December of last year [2006]."

"And where do you live now?"

"In South Carolina."

"And, I mean you're anxious to get back. You have a child who is—has a disability, is that correct?"

The defense did not rise to say that the prosecution was leading the witness.

"Yes, he's autistic," Aspiotis answered.

"I'll try to be fairly crisp with my questioning, but there are some things I want to talk to you about, all right?" said Gullufsen gently.

"Okay," Aspiotis answered easily.

"When you lived here in Alaska did you get to know Mechele Hughes?"

"Yes."

"And how did you get to know her?"

Here it comes . . .

"Through working at the Bush Company. We both worked there together."

"What period of time did you work there, if you recall?"

"'94 through sometime in 1999."

"Did you get to know her outside the Bush Company as well?"

"Yes, I did."

"Describe her for the members of the jury, if you would please."

"My husband and I would go over to what I called Mechele and John's house—it was John's house, but she had moved there, so we spent a lot of time watching movies together and eating and just hanging out in our spare time."

Just two girls hanging out and having a good time . . .

"What was your husband's name?"

"Spiros Aspiotis."

He was a chef at a local Italian restaurant.

"Did you recall, did you have different shifts at the Bush Company or the same shift during the time you were there?"

"The same shifts, you mean day to day?"

"Yes."

"When I first started," Aspiotis told the jury, "it would change a lot. I had to work early, but after I'd been there awhile I got to choose when I worked so . . ."

". . . Did you end up having the same shift or were you there working at the same time as Mechele Hughes?"

"Yes. Uh huh."

"And how would you describe her capability as a dancer at the Bush Company in terms of her ability to make money?"

"I would say that she was one of the top girls that earned a great deal of money."

The jury shifted in their seats.

"What kind of money would we be talking about, say, in a shift?"

Wayne Fricke rose at the defense table.

"Objection as to foundation."

"Overruled," Volland said quickly.

"Can you answer that question?" Gullufsen repeated.

"About how much money?" the former dancer asked.

"Yes."

"Well, I was making in the hundreds, and I think she probably topped that easily."

"Easily?"

"Yeah." Mechele Hughes had some steady customers. "John would come in and TT. I don't know the names of the other guys, but I know John and TT were there."

"John Carlin you mean?"

"Correct."

"And TT would be Kent Leppink?"

"Correct."

"And how about Scott Hilke, was he there very often?"

"He was there probably not as much on a regular basis but yes, he was."

"Before Ms. Hughes moved into John's house in Anchorage, do you know where she was living?"

"Wasilla."

"And were you at that house?"

"Yes, at least once, twice, maybe more a week."

"Sometimes with your husband, sometimes not?"

"Most of the time without my husband because he was working at night and that's usually when I was over there."

"How about when Mechele moved in with John Carlin in south Anchorage, did you spend quite a lot of time there?"

"Yes."

"Did you get to know Kent or TT?"

"Yes, I did."

"And tell us in the context of his being in that circle of people in the house what his relationship was with Mechele."

"Well, from my understanding, TT was under the impression that they were going to get married, so I guess he was her fiancé."

"How did she treat him?"

"Not very well."

"Can you be specific about that?"

"It seemed to me by my observations that TT was just— well, he was a puppet on a string for her. He did everything she asked for."

"How did the troopers get in touch with you?" the prosecutor wondered.

"If I remember correctly, I was the one who contacted them."

At some later point, as the cops were catching up on their interviews, they finally contacted Aspiotis and interviewed her a few times.

"That summer of '96, had you been out of town at all, do you remember?"

"'96 my husband and I went cross-country to North Carolina and then Greece."

"Was there a period of time in early '96 when you were sick and had some surgery?"

"Yes, I had a severe case of endometriosis. I had a laparoscopy to treat it."

Aspiotis would later lend her name to a metaphorical online quilt of women who have suffered through this condition. According to the National Institutes of Health, "Endometriosis occurs when tissues that usually grow inside the uterus instead grow on the outside. These tissues often grow on the surfaces of organs in the pelvis or abdomen, where they are not supposed to grow. A painful though manageable condition, it can be treated through pain medication, hormone therapy or surgery."

"Getting back to Mr. Leppink's—TT's and Mechele's relationship, do you recall any occasions where you all had dinner?"

"A specific . . ."

"At Little Italy when your mother was here."

"Oh yes."

"Who was there?"

"Mechele and Big John and I think Little John. It was table full of people."

"Did your husband cook a big meal for everybody?"

"Yes, he did."

"Was the bill pretty expensive?"

"Yes because it had alcohol and drinks and food."

"At the end of the meal did Kent show up?"

"Yes he did."

"Did Mechele say something to him?"

Fitzgerald rose to his feet.

"Objection as to hearsay."

"It's—" Gullufsen began before being interrupted by Judge Volland.

"To comfort her?" the judge asked.

"It's not for the truth of the matter asserted. It's just—it's a direction."

"I'll allow it," Volland said, and Gullufsen continued his questioning along the same line.

"What did she say to him?"

"She told him to pay for the meal."

"And did he?"

"Yes, he did."

"He didn't ask any questions?"

"No he didn't."

"Do you have any idea how much the bill was?"

"Probably a couple hundred dollars. There was a lot of food and drink consumed."

"Do you recall her asking you about buying life insurance for TT?"

"What I remember about that is when they came in from having gone to get the insurance that she was very, very upset."

"What was she upset about?"

"She told me she got insurance on TT but he wanted to get a policy for her and she didn't—she wasn't happy with that."

Could she have been thinking Leppink had in mind for her the same thing she had in mind for him?

"And how upset did she seem to be by the fact that he wanted her to get insurance on her?"

"Probably the most angry that I'd seen her. Pretty angry, very much beside herself."

"Had she talked to you about buying life insurance for TT before they went out and did it?"

"I think in passing."

"How did John, Big John, treat TT?"

"Not with a lot of respect. Scott and John did [play jokes on TT] a lot."

"Did you and Mechele watch movies a lot?"

Here it comes . . .

"Yes, we did. Uh huh."

"And why is it that you recall a particular movie, watching it with her?"

"Because of what she had said when we were watching the movie."

"Why don't you tell us a little bit about the movie first?"

"The movie is about a woman who's married to a doctor and she had talked him into doing a drug deal, selling pharmaceutical cocaine and he got $470,000. When he's in the shower, she stole the money, took off and went a small town where a young man lived that she met at a bar, and she could tell right away that he was very naïve and hadn't been anywhere else. Just pretty innocent guy, and eventually she talked him into trying to murder her husband for the insurance."

Sounded familiar.

"And how did it end?" asked Gullufsen.

"He ended up in prison and she went free with all the money."

"What did her—what was [Hughes's] reaction to the movie?"

"She just told me *that* was her heroine and that she wanted to be just like her."

The character Bridget Gregory, played absolutely brilliantly by Linda Fiorentino, is an amoral murderess in the same way as Barbara Stanwyck's Phyllis Dietrichson was in *Double Indemnity*.

"Was she talking about the character in the movie or the actress, just to be clear?"

"She was talking about the character in the movie itself."

"Do you recall if there were other people who watched this with you?"

"No, I don't recall. Don't think so."

But Gullufsen had established in the jury's mind the possibility that Linehan/Hughes had used the plot of *The Last Seduction*, which so far had not been named, to carry out the murder of Kent Leppink.

"Do you recall her traveling to Europe at all?"

"Yes."

"What do you recall about that?"

"She went to Amsterdam with John."

There was more testimony from Aspiotis establishing that

Hughes treated Leppink like a piece of crap left out in the sun too long. But Gullufsen had another ace up his sleeve.

"Did you keep a diary during this period of time?"

"Yes, I did."

"And the court reviewed your diary and provided both sides with copies?"

"Yes."

"Did you put everything in your diary?"

"No."

"There would be a lot that you didn't put in your diary?"

"Objection to leading," shouted Fitzgerald.

"Overruled," Volland said and prompted the witness to continue.

"There is—it depended on my mood and if I felt like . . . at times I was too busy to think about even writing in any journal, so it just depended on the mood I was in and what I was doing."

"Did you—did there come an end to your relationship with Mechele?"

"Yes."

"And how did that come about?"

"Well, I finally—after being around her so long I just got tired of the web that she had woven and the deceit and the manipulation and the lies," Aspiotis responded eloquently.

"Did you actually call her and end it?"

"Yes, yes I did."

"When did that happen?"

"I believe it was in February that it happened."

"Is that reflected in your diary?"

"Yes, it's in there."

The judge gave her original copies of the diary to identify the date since Gullufsen was making a point of pinning it down.

"Yeah, there's quite a bit here. Yeah, that's February 27th."
That was the date she ended her relationship with Hughes.

"Did you tell her why?"

"Yes, I did."

That must have been quite a conversation.

CHAPTER

15

The prosecuting attorney continued his cross.

"Did you have any contact with her after that?"

"No I didn't."

"Did you come to know Little John that is John Carlin IV?"

"Yes, I did."

"And tell the members of the jury, how that relationship developed; how close did it get?"

"Well, Little John would come over to our apartment and my husband and I would talk to him and hang out with him."

"Did he ever stay overnight?"

"I don't think so. I don't recall."

"All right. Thank you m'am. I have no further questions."

"Okay," said Aspiotis, shifting in the witness box.

"Mr. Fitzgerald?" the judge asked.

"Thank you judge," and Fitzgerald rose for the cross.

"Good afternoon," said Fitzgerald affably. "Is it Ms. Aspiotis?"

"Yes."

"M'am prior to today we have not met, have we?"

"No."

"And I made a phone call to you last night after I was provided your number for the first time. Do you remember that phone call?"

Aspiotis did.

"And I asked if you'd be willing to speak with me? And I didn't pressure you did I?"

"Yes. And no, you didn't."

"You declined that invitation as is your prerogative."

"Correct."

"And I think what you said you would rather not speak to me because what you could say to me might be used against you. Do you remember that?"

"I believe I said it wasn't advantageous of me to speak to you."

That was a smart way of saying something without using an expletive.

"And that you preferred to speak with me here in the courtroom?"

"Correct."

Interesting roll of the dice. Mano a mano, the former stripper against the defense attorney for the former stripper.

"Can you tell the jury how many times you might have talked to Mr. Gullufsen or any of the investigators associated with this case?"

"Wow. I don't know. Quite a few—quite a few times, yes."

"You continued to provide them information during the course of your relationship with them, correct?"

"Correct."

"And the diary that we were just speaking about was produced today, is that right?"

"To you?"

"Your honor, I'd like to approach," said Gullufsen from the prosecution table.

"Please," said the courtly judge.

Gullufsen changed his mind. "Strike that judge."

And Fitzgerald shot back to the witness in the box, "You indicated that you first met Ms. Hughes now Mrs. Linehan while you were dancing at the Bush Company."

"Correct."

"And when did you start dancing at the Bush Company, do you remember?"

"Sometime in '94."

"And then did you also dance elsewhere?"

"Yes, I have."

"And where was it that you danced?"

"At PJ's in Spenard and Las Vegas at Cheetah's and the Palomino Club."

These were higher-class strip joints.

"And what have your dance names been?"

Like Hughes, who used Bobbi Jo as her dance name, Aspiotis had hers; Fitzgerald had done his research well.

"Zoe and Alyson and Mystique."

The last was a movie reference too, to the character played by Rebecca Romijn in *X-Men* (2000).

"And how long, about, have you been a dancer?"

"Collectively probably six years."

"With respect to this notion of how much Ms. Hughes was making, you never counted out how much she was making nightly, did you?"

"Correct."

"And the club itself took a cut did it not?"

"A percentage."

"Was it on a percentage basis or was it on an hourly basis in how was it determined?"

"We tipped out whatever we felt like they deserved that—

for the night or whatever—I couldn't tell you percent, I really don't know."

"Fair enough. It depended on whether you were tipping out, for instance, the DJ, the bouncer, the—"

"Uh huh."

"The folks working behind the bar?"

"Right."

"And you indicated that you had seen a couple of individuals in which you characterized as I understand, as regular customers for Ms. Hughes."

"Correct."

"And those included John Carlin, right?"

"Yes, yes."

"And Kent Leppink?"

"Yes."

"And when you go to dance at a place like that, you spend a portion of the time on the stage right?"

"Correct."

"And then you can give lap dances, right?"

"Correct."

"And you can also sit down and socialize with regular customers or other customers, right?"

"Yes."

"And with regard to Ms. Hughes those regular customers whether they be regular customers or customers that would come in, I mean, these were folks that were willingly providing money for the show they were getting right?"

"Yes."

"It was entertainment, right?"

"Yes."

"And with regard to Ms. Hughes, typically, as I understand your statement, Ms. Hughes didn't do a lot of dancing. She did a lot of socializing. But not a lot of dancing?"

"Yes."

"And you were a little bit jealous about that, were you not?"

"No."

"Well, didn't you think that it was somewhat unfair to the customer if Ms. Hughes was just socializing with them rather than dancing for them?"

"No."

"Didn't you indicate do you have your statement up there M'am?"

"Yes," said Aspiotis, looking down at her notes.

"And then you made a comment [in her diary] with regard to, well, the customer expects something for their money, right, as far as dancers go right?"

"Right."

"And you couldn't conceive that clients would pay to, for instance socialize with her, right?"

"Could you repeat that?"

"You couldn't conceive that most—that men would just sit there and talk to her, right?"

"It's been done."

"Well indeed, maybe not the most enlightened view of men, but didn't you indicate most of the men aren't willing to just sit there and pay the girls to talk for hours, right?"

"Correct."

"But that's what Ms. Hughes was doing. She didn't really like to dance."

"I don't know."

The truth was, most dancers don't "like" to dance; they do it for big money. They like the money. Like the Shadow, they have the power to cloud men's minds, only they don't do it with Eastern mysticism. They do it with bodies that men fantasize about and ultimately want to own for themselves.

The next few minutes of court time deteriorated into an argument between Fitzgerald, who wanted to introduce a porn video that Aspiotis had watched with Carlin III, and the prosecutor. It had to do with a general statement Aspiotis had given during her grand jury testimony, something to the effect that "men like porno tapes."

Hardly a surprise.

"If I understood you correctly," Fitzgerald was allowed to say after all the wrangling, "you guys watched a pornographic film. You did that because Mechele wouldn't let you do that when she was there. You 'wanted him [John] to have a good time and we were just, you know, having fun.'"

"Correct."

"With regard to the comment guys like that stuff, what you were referencing was that men liked porn videos, right?"

"I also thought that it was funny."

Moving to the Wasilla house and the strange living arrangements there, Fitzgerald said, "As I understood your direct testimony, you indicated that you were over there what, a couple times a week?"

"Yeah, probably."

"And you said you didn't like the way Mechele treated Kent Leppink, is that right?"

"Correct."

"You described him as kind of an errand boy?"

"Yes."

"And everybody in the house kind of treated him that way, right?"

"Well, my husband didn't."

"But you weren't living in the house, were you?"

"Well, true."

"So everybody in the house that was living there treated him pretty much same way."

"Yes."

"Did Mr. Leppink ever complain to you that he believed that he was being mistreated at that house?"

"Yeah, I don't think he used those words verbatim, but—"

"Do you know where he lived prior to the time that he was actually living at the Carlin residence?"

"I don't recall."

"Did he ever mention to you at any time that he lived with Russ Williams and his wife Shirley?"

"No."

Fitzgerald turned back to the Wasilla house.

"Was Mr. Leppink living in the Wasilla house as best you know?"

"It's hard to say because—no, I don't think so. I don't think so."

"Were you aware whether he would leave for days at a time and then return to that house?"

"He would leave for days at a time, yes."

"Isn't that something that Ms. Hughes talked to you about, that Mr. Leppink would just leave for days at a time?"

"I don't recall."

Fitzgerald had tried to break Aspiotis without success.

Gullufsen finished the prosecution's case and sat down. Most of the defense's case consisted of character witnesses, testifying to Linehan's new life. Despite what the defense said, it wasn't much of a case. The note seemed to be incontrovertible evidence that Hughes had conspired to kill Leppink with Carlin as the triggerman.

The defense did little or nothing, to puncture that theory. The prosecution and defense delivered their closing statements. Volland charged the jury and they filed out to their deliberations.

October 24, 2007

The jury filed into the courtroom, not a wet eye among them. They handed the verdict sheet to the court clerk, who passed it up to the judge. He looked at it a moment.

"Would the defendant please rise?"

Along with her husband and lawyers, Linehan rose to hear the verdict. The verdict slip was handed from the foreman to the court clerk, who then gave it to the judge, who unfolded it.

"The jury has convicted you of first-degree murder," Volland pronounced.

Mechele Hughes didn't even flinch. Colin Linehan slumped at the words. Friends and family members of the convicted killer started to cry. The verdict was read; Colin Linehan knelt next to his wife, who had sat back down. In his grief, he buried his head in her shoulder. The deputies allowed husband and wife a last embrace. Then they slapped on the cuffs and escorted her from the courtroom.

Soon it would be time for sentencing, but not before various presentencing motions, a sentencing report, and a lot of other things that took the conclusion of the case into 2008. Would Linehan get the same sentence as Carlin? No one knew.

April 3, 2008

Mechele Linehan was finally going to face her sentence for killing Kent Leppink. The question was if the judge, like so many men before him, would fall to her charms and give her a lighter sentence. Considering her history with men, it was more than possible.

During the sentencing phase, both the Leppink and Linehan families were allowed to address the court before the final sentence was rendered. Dr. Colin Linehan was grasping at straws to stop his beloved wife and the mother of his child from spending the rest of her life behind bars for a murder he was sure she had not committed. At the defense table, dressed in orange prison garb, Mechele Linehan watched as her husband took the stand.

Linehan decided to go the emotional route with a little bit of empathy thrown in. Betsy and Ransom Leppink were in the courtroom, listening as he spoke softly.

"I'm 36 years old and Kent was 36 years old. He was a brother, friend, son," he said, looking at them. "There's nothing more precious than a human life. It kills me that in their hearts they think that Mechele had anything to do with that. Because I know from the bottom of my heart and soul that she did not."

Gullufsen was on his feet.

"Objection!"

The judge instructed the jury to ignore the last remark. Innocence was not relevant during sentencing because the jury had rendered its verdict. Sentencing was about mitigating circumstances and, sometimes, justice, depending on whose side you are on. So Linehan obeyed the court and began a recitation of Linehan's life post-Alaska.

He said that she was a generous woman who worked hard for family, friends, and anyone who employed her. He emphasized her master's degree in public administration, as if this was something a murderer would never get.

Linehan claimed that they did not meet at a strip club. They actually met, he said, in 1997 at a New Orleans park, where she went regularly to run with her dogs. She was a student at Loyola University, he said, and he was a physician at Tulane University. Now he was a family doctor at a Washington State army base. Then he appealed to the jurors' tear ducts, concentrating on their family in Olympia and their eight-year-old daughter who would be without her mother if she went to jail. He said they had just started a cosmetic clinic business.

In the courtroom, the Leppink and Linehan/Hughes families listened intently. They had taken to avoiding each other during the trial. Linehan's statement to them produced no noticeable emotional effect. But would Mechele Linehan, aka Hughes, move the judge with her statement? She had not testified on her behalf, as Carlin hadn't (defendants rarely do in murder trials). The defendant, though a convicted murderer, did have the right to address the court before sentencing, and she did.

At the defense table, Mechele Linehan rose to address the judge who held her future in his hands. Leniency was on everyone's mind, if she were successful. After all, her supporters reasoned, it was circumstantial evidence that convicted her, right? Surely the judge would take that into consideration.

"I have not lived a life of greed, manipulation or that of a fictional character of a Hollywood movie," said the thirty-five-year-old who was convicted of murdering for money. She described herself as a happy wife and mother to a young daughter, someone who enjoyed renovating her old Olympia, Washington, home and having homemade pizza parties.

"I beg you, from the bottom of my heart, to allow me the chance to go back to my family," she said.

"I am not the monster I have been made out to be," insisting instead she was a good woman caught in unusual circumstances, which she got out of and made a good life for herself. In her five-minute statement, Mechele Linehan claimed that as a dancer at the Bush, she made "poor choices." Yes, she accepted gifts and money from men, including Leppink, whom she met at the bar. But that was "then" and this is "now."

She sat down and waited. After a pause, Superior Court Judge Philip Volland addressed her directly.

"You are a cold-hearted killer. The murder of Kent Leppink was a heinous crime. In my mind I can find no principled distinction between the puppet who pulls the trigger and the puppeteer who pulls the strings," Volland said of Linehan's role. "And in my judgment, Ms. Linehan was the puppeteer who pulled the strings."

Volland deduced that there are "two Linehans" in one body. She was a seductive manipulator who charmed many, especially men. He sided with the prosecution and handed down the maximum sentence, ninety-nine years, saying Linehan's young daughter wouldn't likely be seeing her mother outside of a prison until she was well into her own adulthood. Linehan will be first eligible for parole in thirty-three years.

The stripper killer showed no emotion as the sentence was handed down. Judge Volland allowed her husband, Colin Linehan, "one final embrace" before deputies led her into the labyrinth of the courthouse and the prison system to begin her sentence. Outside the courtroom, Dr. Linehan said, "There's the Mechele that everyone who knows her and has been around her for years knows. And the Mechele that the prosecution invented, their narrative. We will appeal vigorously the decisions by Judge Volland during the trial."

The Leppink family felt differently.

"I feel that God has a way of answering crimes," Betsy Leppink said.

Holding hands with husband, Kenneth, she made it clear that the sentence did not bring the closure her family needs.

"Only if we could walk home with our son could it be over."

September 2008

In the "Statement of Points on Appeal," Linehan's appeals lawyers stated that they intended to rely on the following points on appeal:

The trial court allowed references and evidence to be introduced regarding the movie "Last Seduction" over objection.

The trial court refused to allow impeachment of witness L. Aspiotis to be perfected demonstrating she perjured herself during her trial testimony.

The trial court allowed admission of evidence of financial information about Mechele Linehan over objection.

The trial court allowed admission of observations about Mechele Linehan over objection.

The trial court allowed admission of certain interaction between Mechele Linehan and men over objection.

The trial court allowed admission of Mechele Linehan's receipt of gifts, money and jewelry from men over objection.

The trial court permitted a bank official to opine that Mechele Linehan had forged a check over objection.

The trial court permitted an allegory about a turtle/scorpion over objection.

The trial court permitted the prosecutor to use the absence of e-mails prior to March, 2007 as a sword during his closing argument, while objecting to the admissibility of the same as irrelevant earlier.

That was a lot for an appeals court to consider, especially considering the defense was asking the appeals court to throw out the prosecution's entire case. Not likely to happen in a conservative state like Alaska where ninety-nine years means ninety-nine years. Hope, though, springs eternal.

The appeals document continues:

The trial court permitted cross-examination of Dr. Colin Linehan in a manner that suggested that Dr. Linehan had improperly prescribed medications.

The trial court permitted conversations between Brian Brundin and Kent Leppink as "state of mind," over objection as both hearsay/relevance.

The trial court permitted admission of the Hope note over objection.

The trial court precluded introduction of various comments by Mechele Linehan.

The trial court allowed the admission of John Carlin IV's testimony regarding alleged post-incident misconduct.

The trial court allowed admission of e-mail communications between John Carlin III and other persons absent adequate foundation.

The trial court precluded the defense from full and fair cross-examination of numerous witnesses.

The trial court denied the motion to preclude "flight" evidence.

The trial court denied the motion to exclude as hearsay the statements of John Carlin III.

The trial court denied the objection to the introduction of Rule 404(b) evidence, including the post-incident gun washing.

The trial court denied the motion to exclude hearsay in violation of the applicable rules and constitutional protections, including the letters from Kent Leppink to his parents.

The trial court denied the motion to exclude statements by John Carlin III.

The trial court denied the motion to exclude statements made by Kent Leppink regarding gifts and money.

The trial court denied the motion to suppress search/seizure of the Gateway laptop computer or *de novo* review of the same.

The trial court denied the motion to exclude reference to Mechele Linehan's past.

The trial court's sentence of 99 years is excessive.

The last point was probably the one on which Mechele Hughes could hang her hat. Ninety-nine years for conspiracy to commit murder did seem rather steep to some. But to those who knew Kent Leppink as a kind, gentle soul who made the world a better place with his presence, it wasn't excessive at all. Ultimately, of course, it was for the courts to decide.

"The appeal is in its early stages," explained one of her appeal attorneys, "and she will file a brief. We will then have an opportunity to respond. Then they get to have an opportunity to respond again, and we do too. Either side can ask for oral arguments. If that happens, a decision can take six months to a year from the time the court has all the information. If there are no oral arguments, the time frame would be shorter. We're looking well into 2009 before any decision."

Mechele—she's not talking—is doing something to get herself out faster than even the last famous convicted Alaskan murderer could ever have conceived in his brilliant brain. His name was Robert Stroud, aka "The Birdman of Alcatraz."

According to the site, it "is run by friends and family of Mechele Linehan." The site is "devoted to positive sharing on the journey to true justice." This is an interactive true crime book. Turn around and go to your computer and type in freemechele.blogspot.com.

While the site states that Linehan was convicted of "conspiring to murder Kent Leppink," with that out of the way, Mechele's friends and family have been kind enough to provide a link to an online store selling various products, including T-shirts, mugs, stickers, pins, and mouse pads emblazoned with the words "Free Me! Mechele Linehan is innocent."

Prices vary. Sometimes a sweat shirt was selling for $30.99, while you could get a tank top for $29.99. Linehan products are priced higher than similar ones at Hollister's and other "name" retail stores. They carry the Hollister name on them instead of "Free Me! Mechele Linehan is innocent."

One of the updates at Mechele's blog, dated Sunday, July 7, 2008, was as follows:

LEGAL DEFENSE FUND FOR MECHELE

Mechele's Mom, Sandy McWilliams, is starting a legal defense fund for her. She will be posting more particulars about the fund soon. If you would like to help support Mechele's legal defense, you can donate using PayPal with the button here or on the sidebar (a percentage of your donation will be taken by PayPal fees.)

It was, arguably, one of the greatest examples of chutzpah in criminal justice: the convicted murder who is convicted by society then asking that same society to finance her appeal, while said society is fighting to keep her in jail. Taxpayers do not finance murderers' appeals. Since Hughes had nothing legally to do with the site, the First Amendment allowed her friends to post the information.

That such a site could exist is tribute to the American Constitution and the Founding Fathers. It is, however, doubtful that any of them, with the exception of Benjamin Franklin, would have contributed to Mechele Hughes's defense fund.

There was no doubt, however, that a man would always be by Mechele Hughes's side.

Epilogue

The Kenai Peninsula is still a very dangerous place. Up until August 2008, there were eighteen deaths caused by grizzly bear mauling. It's a place where you really have to watch yourself and pay attention to where you are, especially if you're in prison.

Now if you're in prison, there are a few rules. First and foremost, if someone hits you, you hit back with something bigger and harder. To not retaliate for a physical attack in prison is absolute suicide because from that point onward, every prisoner knows he can fuck with you and there'll be no retribution. That's how guys turn into "bitches."

The idea, then, is if you are ambushed, for example, and beat up, when you come back from the infirmary, you *don't* go into protective custody. You don't ask for it, you don't look for it, especially if you are going to be there a long, long time. What you do is pick up a chair and hit the guy on the head who beat the shit out of you and give him a concussion. Then you turn around and take that same chair and hit the guy who held you while guy number one beat you. Hit him across the jaw and shatter it.

At that point, the prison will be like a riot in a Warner

Bros. thirties gangster movie. You'll get beat up by the guards and go to the hole for a while—yes, they still call isolation "the hole"—because you dared to send a message. But once you get out of the hole, no one will mess with you . . . ever. All this is known, and known quickly, by anyone who finds himself in prison anywhere.

Spring Creek Correctional Institution was located on the banks of the appropriately named Resurrection Bay, on the scenic but isolated southwestern coastline of the Kenai Peninsula, the place was built by the state of Alaska in 1988 to house maximum security prisoners. Spring Creek resembles "Oz," the fictional prison in the HBO series.

It was here that John Carlin III was sent to serve his life sentence. Carlin's pod contained sixty convicts housed in two-man cells. There was also a common meeting area. Locked in every night in their two-man cells, the prisoners felt one day blend into another. Some, like Carlin, had hope.

"I didn't do it," Carlin told one and all who would ask, especially this one TV show, *Vapid and Vacuous*, which ran on one of the networks. *V&V* did an episode about the case. When it was rerun in August 2008, some of Carlin's fellow prisoners took offense at his celebrity and made it a point to rearrange his features.

"There are some people here who didn't like the way I looked, so I got a prison makeover of sorts," Carlin III wrote eloquently.

Instead of beating the crap out of the people who beat him up, Carlin allowed the warden to put him into protective custody; he didn't like it. An avid reader of history and biography, he checked Winston Churchill's *A History of the English Speaking Peoples* out of the prison library and took it along for company. But even Churchill's prose didn't occupy his time well enough.

"Living in the hole here is somewhat like living in the primate section of the zoo," he wrote, once again eloquently, and asked to be transferred back into the general prison population.

The request was granted. Carlin was put back into the general prison population.

It was at 11 P.M. on Monday, October 27, 2008, that Preston Wade got the call. There'd been a "disturbance" at the prison in Seward. John Carlin III was on his way by ambulance to Providence Seward Hospital. When he got there, he was pronounced dead on arrival (DOA). Prisoners had decided to rearrange his features for good; they had beaten him to death.

Carlin's death is only the second homicide to ever occur within the state's prisons. The first was in 2004, also at Spring Creek, when convicted killer Carl Abuhl strangled his cellmate, Gregory Beaudoin. When the homicide of Carlin occurred, Alaska's governor, Sarah Palin, was in the middle of her vice presidential campaign and made no comment. But at Linehan's Web site, there was much grieving, with sympathetic posts from the people who run the site, anonymous posters, and Carlin's own son.

"A travesty of justice," was the way he described it, believing his father to be firmly innocent despite his testimony at both trials to the contrary. He would not speculate as to his theory of the crime, but it made no difference. His father was dead, he'd testified against him, and he would have to live with it.

"Death ends a life but it doesn't end a relationship which struggles on in the survivor's mind toward some final resolution it never finds," wrote playwright Robert Anderson in his play *I Never Sang for My Father.*

Acknowledgments

Interviews, official court documents, and research from an extensive amount of verifiable online sources have all been used in the writing of this book. Former Wasilla chief of police Irl Stambaugh and current Wasilla sergeant Jean Achee were particularly kind and helpful. Not so the State of Alaska and the Alaskan State Police, who refused to cooperate in the writing of this book.

After a request in writing for an interview with Alaskan cold case squad investigator Jim Stogsdill, he replied in writing. "Linehan has filed an appeal regarding her conviction. That limits the amount and kind of information I can offer. If you contact Pat Gullufsen, prosecutor, he may not have the same restrictions I have."

After a failed attempt to communicate using Dr. Bell's invention, I still asked him in a subsequent e-mail follow-up, "Why didn't the troopers back in 1996–1997 go for an indictment of Hughes and Carlin? And why was this case number one on the cold case squad's agenda? Could you also give me some background on the Alaska Cold Case Squad?"

Mr. Stogsdill did not reply to that request. Pat Gullufsen's reply to my humble interview request was also to
decline. Court documents and many of the police reports
were available from the Alaskan court system, and my re-
searcher, Janaan Kitchen, got them. Full transcripts were
not available from either trial. Taken together, though, the
public evidence of the case provides an inside look at how
this case really transpired over time, and really across a
continent.

Some of the questions the lawyers asked at trial are re-
constructed here on the basis of the witness's answers in
the partial transcripts. Names have been changed to protect
the innocent, especially people on the periphery of the case
whose privacy does not need to be intruded upon. Any simi-
larity between the fictitious names used here and real names
is totally coincidental.

Because the Leppink murder investigation spread across
the millennium, not to mention state lines, some scenes
are presented slightly out of order. The major detectives on
the case—there were many—have been combined into one
person to simplify the narrative. Preston Wade is a combination of all the fine detectives in Alaska who worked
on the "black widow murder," with the kind of intelligence
and due diligence not only to the law but to Kent Leppink's
very-much-alive memory.

It is absolute coincidence that Sarah Palin figured in this
story during one of the most passionate elections in U.S. history. While reading a copy of the interview with Hughes in
Wasilla by the police in 1996, I looked up at the TV screen
to see John McCain announce Palin as his vice presidential pick. As a journalist, it was incumbent upon me to investigate her involvement in the Leppink murder since she
was Wasilla's mayor during the key part of the 1996–1997
murder investigation. With due diligence to what Carl Bern-

stein defines as journalism—"the best obtainable version of the truth"—that information is presented here.

In addition to Ms. Kitchen to whom I owe a debt of gratitude for her impeccable research and organization, Wayne Fricke in Washington State, one of Ms. Linehan's attorneys, kindly provided insight from his perspective. Kevin Verpent gave valuable advice. While John Carlin IV did not sit for an interview, he was kind enough to answer my e-mails like a gentleman. I wish him well.

Most of all, Will Hinton, my brilliant young editor, did what he always does—edit with thought and insight.

Shocking true accounts of murder Texas-style from

KATHRYN CASEY

A DESCENT INTO HELL
THE TRUE STORY OF AN ALTAR BOY, A CHEERLEADER, AND A TWISTED TEXAS MURDER
978-0-06-123087-5

The gripping true story of one of the most brutal slayings in University of Texas history.

DIE, MY LOVE
A TRUE STORY OF REVENGE, MURDER, AND TWO TEXAS SISTERS
978-0-06-084620-6

When college professor Fred Jablin was found dead in his driveway, police immediately turned their attention to his ex-wife—who had lost a bitter custody battle.

SHE WANTED IT ALL
A TRUE STORY OF SEX, MURDER, AND A TEXAS MILLIONAIRE
978-0-06-056764-4

Trophy wife Celeste Beard wasn't satisfied with a luxurious lifestyle and her rich Austin media mogul husband's devotion—so she took his life!

A WARRANT TO KILL
A TRUE STORY OF OBSESSION, LIES AND A KILLER COP
978-0-380-78041-9

Problems had always followed Susan White, but when she remarried and moved to Houston's posh suburbs, she thought the past was behind her—until she met a deputy sheriff named Kent McGowen who would soon become her worst nightmare.